Mordecai Richler

Twayne's World Authors Series

Canadian Literature

Robert Lecker, Editor

McGill University

TWAS 707

MORDECAI RICHLER
(1931–   )
Photograph courtesy of COM/MEDIA,
University of Calgary.

Mordecai Richler

By Victor J. Ramraj

University of Calgary

Twayne Publishers • *Boston*

Mordecai Richler

Victor J. Ramraj

Copyright © 1983 by G. K. Hall & Company
All Rights Reserved
Published by Twayne Publishers
A Division of G. K. Hall & Company
70 Lincoln Street
Boston, Massachusetts 02111

Book Production by John Amburg

Book Design by Barbara Anderson

Printed on permanent/durable acid-free
paper and bound in the United States of
America.

Library of Congress Cataloging in Publication Data

Ramraj, Victor J.
    Mordecai Richler.

    (Twayne's world authors series; TWAS 707)
    Bibliography: p. 143
    Includes index.
    1. Richler, Mordecai, 1931–   .—Criticism
and interpretation.   I. Title.   II. Series.
PR9199.3.R5Z84   1983   813'.54   83-10668
ISBN 0-8057-6554-9

To Victor and Sharon

Contents

About the Author

Victor J. Ramraj received his degrees from the University of London and the University of New Brunswick. He has taught at the University of New Brunswick and at the University of Calgary, where he now offers courses in his two areas of interest: Canadian and Commonwealth Literature. Dr. Ramraj has published articles on several Canadian and Commonwealth writers in North American, Caribbean, and European journals.

Preface

Mordecai Richler is unquestionably one of Canada's foremost contemporary writers. Though he is preeminently a novelist, he has acquired a reputation as a controversial journalist who is outspoken, unequivocal, and censorious. These qualities are certainly evident in several of his journalistic pieces and have come to be associated in the public imagination with his writing. However, they are not the dominant characteristics of his fiction. In his novels—on which I focus in this study—Richler exhibits an acutely ambivalent perception of life, and I intend to show that this is the source of his strength and, to a lesser extent, of his weakness as a novelist.

Richler's binary vision fosters in his fiction an encompassing, ironic, enquiring approach to human experience. His tone, fluctuating between sympathy and censure imbues his work with an energizing tension. His protagonists, themselves ambivalent beings, simultaneously love and hate, accept and reject particular individuals, ideas, and places, and try to come to grips with their often tormenting contradictory feelings. They attempt quests for self-knowledge that follow a dialectic course and have no clear resolutions.

In the opening chapter, I examine in a preliminary way Richler's ambivalence and its artistic consequences. Here also I tentatively explore its origin in the author's personal experiences. In subsequent chapters I provide, as far as space allows, a detailed descriptive-analytical study of each novel in a loosely chronological order, which conveniently facilitates tracing Richler's development as a novelist while allowing the novels to be paired advantageously by subject matter and tone. In these chapters, my emphasis is two-fold: to provide an introductory survey of Richler's fiction and to show that his ambivalence is the central and unifying factor in his work.

The passages from Mordecai Richler's books are quoted with the kind permission of his publishers, McClelland and Stewart, Toronto. I should like to express my gratitude to Mr. Mordecai Richler for taking the time to discuss his work with me and for permitting me to quote from his manuscripts in the Mordecai Richler Papers at the University of Calgary Library. I am indebted to the late Dr. Desmond Pacey for his assistance in the early stages of this study; to Dr. Saad El-Gabalawy and Dr. Roderick McGillis for their useful comments; to Mrs. Jean Tener and Mrs. Polly Steele of the University of Calgary Library for their assistance with the Mordecai Richler Papers; to the University of Calgary for a research grant to work on this study; to Mrs. Joyce Kee and Mrs. Barbara McQuaid for generously typing and proofing my manuscript; and to my wife for her constant and invaluable support.

Victor J. Ramraj

University of Calgary

Chronology

1931 Born 27 January, in Montreal, Quebec, to Moses and Lily Richler.

1936–1946 Attended United Talmud Torah and Baron Byng High School, Montreal.

1944 Parents divorced; assisted mother with her Laurentian summer resort.

1948–1950 Attended Sir George Williams College, Montreal; worked part-time as reporter for the *Montreal Herald*.

1951 Traveled to London, Paris, Spain. First published short story, "Shades of Darkness," in *Points*. Began work on *The Acrobats*.

1952 Returned to Canada; joined Canadian Broadcasting Corporation in Montreal as a radio news editor.

1954 *The Acrobats*. Left Canada to reside in London, accompanied by Catherine Boudreau from whom, after a brief marriage, he was divorced.

1955 *Son of a Smaller Hero*.

1957 *A Choice of Enemies*.

1959 *The Apprenticeship of Duddy Kravitz*. Awarded Canada Council Junior Arts Fellowship and the University of Western Ontario President's Medal for best general article published in Canada.

1960 Married Florence Wood. Awarded second Canada Council Junior Arts Fellowship.

1961 Awarded Guggenheim Foundation Fellowship in Creative Writing.

1963 *The Incomparable Atuk*.

1967 Father died. Awarded Canada Council Senior Arts Fellowship.

1968 *Cocksure* and *Hunting Tigers Under Glass*. These won the Governor-General's Literary Award. Writer-in-Residence at Sir George Williams University, Montreal. Awarded *Paris Review* annual prize for humor.

1969   *The Street.*

1970   *Canadian Writing Today.*

1971   *St. Urbain's Horseman.* This novel won the Governor-General's Literary Award.

1972   *Shovelling Trouble.* Returned with family to live in Montreal. Visiting Professor, English Department, Carleton University, Ottawa, until 1974.

1974   *Notes on an Endangered Species.* Scripted film of *The Apprenticeship of Duddy Kravitz.* Sold his papers (to 1973) to the University of Calgary Library.

1975   *Jacob Two-Two Meets the Hooded Fang.*

1976   Appointed to the Editorial Board of the Book of the Month Club. Awarded first annual Ruth Schwartz Children's Book Award.

1977   *Images of Spain.*

1980   *Joshua Then and Now.*

Chapter One
Introduction: Ambivalent Vision

The protagonists of Mordecai Richler's fiction constantly find themselves faced with situations in which they experience simultaneously or alternatingly opposed attitudes and feelings toward people, places, or ideas—a human response for which Eugene Bleuler coined the term *ambivalency*.[1] Like his protagonists, with whom he is often closely identified, Richler himself exhibits a profoundly ambivalent vision of life which is at the very core of his artistic being and conditions his perception and depiction of experience. His ambivalence shows itself in various ways: in his simultaneous acceptance and rejection of the Montreal Jewish society of his childhood and youth; in his tendency to mock and at the same time to accommodate human shortcomings; in his concurrent tolerance and censure of rogues like Duddy Kravitz, whom, he has admitted, he both admires and despises;[2] and in his conscious effort to be both a moral, "serious" novelist and an entertainer—two functions he regards as being antithetical to each other.[3]

Richler's ambivalence informs not just his treatment of themes and characters but his narrative, structure, and tone, and even the antithetical turn of certain sentences as well. His fiction is intensely ironic and displays a vitalizing ambiguity that works against facile answers and dogmatic resolutions. The narrative and structure of his novels generally take the form of unfulfilled quests which follow a dialectic progression. His response to man's shortcomings, wavering between censure and acceptance, reduces the cogency of whatever satirical pieces he attempts, and serves to complicate his tone to such an extent that critics are divided in evaluating even his more censorious works as satires proper. Ambivalence sometimes works against an artist, and certain minor weaknesses in Richler's fiction are attributable to his bifocal vision. His novels are untidily structured, sometimes with alternating episodes and inset scenes revealing jarringly

inconsistent observations, styles, and tones. And the reader occasionally becomes frustrated by his indecisive protagonists' inability to
make much progress in their various emotional and mental labyrinths.

Ambivalent Author

A third-generation Canadian Jew, Mordecai Richler straddled as a
youth the traditional, orthodox life of his immigrant grandparents
and the more assimilationist, less rigid attitude of later generations
born in North America. His grandfather (whose name, "Reichler,"
was inadvertently misspelled by an immigration officer) ventured to
Canada by steerage in 1904 to escape the Eastern European pogroms
and settled with other Jewish immigrants in the impoverished east
end of Montreal. Richler was born into a world rigidly circumscribed
by orthodoxy and by fear and ignorance of French and English Canadians. Very much a part of this narrow, self-contained society initially, he attended Jewish parochial school, studied the Talmud and
Modern Hebrew, and was expected to become a rabbi. Parochial
schooling, ironically, opened his eyes to the world beyond the Jewish
ghetto. The time spent there was for him "a mixed pleasure,"[4] but,
more significantly, it was the germinating point of a sensibility aptly
described by him as being "armed with a double hook."[5] He was exposed to old, conservative teachers of Hebrew as well as to young female English-language instructors who were "charming, bracingly
modern and concerned about our future. They told us about El Cam-
pesino, how John Steinbeck wrote the truth, and read Sacco's speech
to the court aloud to us."[6]

Richler began easing away from orthodoxy while still at parochial
school, and continued to do so while attending Baron Byng High
School, which, though it had a student body almost totally Jewish,
was under the jurisdiction of the Protestant School Board of Montreal. Here, as he states in the Foreword to The Street, he became further aware of the non-Jewish world,[7] and began to conceive of himself
as both Jewish and Canadian. This was not always an easy comple-
mentary conception of himself. Exposed to the real and the imagined
prejudices and resentments of Jews on the one hand and of French
and English Canadians on the other, he found being Jewish and Canadian at times virtually antithetical. "The minority man," he points
out, quoting Norman Mailer, "grows up with a double-image of
himself, his own and society's" (ST, 83). One of the more disturbing

instances of this in Richler's youthful experience was his response to John Buchan's *The Thirty-Nine Steps:*

As badly as I wanted to identify with Richard Hannay, two-fisted soldier of fortune, I couldn't without betraying myself. My grandfather, *pace* Buchan, went in fear of being flogged in some one-horse location on the Volga, which was why we were in Canada. However, I owe to Buchan the image of my grandfather as a little white-faced Jew with an eye like a rattlesnake. It is an image I briefly responded to, alas, if only because Hannay, so obviously on the side of good, accepted it without question. (*ST,* 83)

His community's "split loyalties"[8] to Canada and the United States further complicated Richler's early life. Exposed to British and American influences in sports, entertainment, and literature, his community was proud of visiting British Shakespeare Companies and that the better-known Canadian writers, Stephen Leacock for instance, were writing within a British tradition. But they also felt a kinship with Americans, saw American sports heroes and entertainers as theirs, and believed New York to be their true capital. Initially, they admired also the German and Austrian Jewish war refugees who settled in Montreal's east end, considering these newcomers to be far more sophisticated and better educated than themselves. Yet they were cut to the quick and ready to defend Canada when these refugees snobbishly found Canadian culture thin, Montreal provincial, and the local Jews narrow-minded.

After high school, Richler wanted to attend McGill University. His marks, however, were not good enough, and he settled for Sir George Williams College, which he attended for two years as an English major. Several first-year courses he found quite elementary and uninspiring. These were often butts of his early satirical pieces. It was here, nevertheless, that affable professors and older students introduced him to music, opera, and the poetry of Eliot, cummings, and Auden. Yet, eventually, afraid of being enmeshed and devitalized by academic life, he abandoned college for the wider world. His attitude to academe has always been mixed. Academic figures in his novels, such as Theo Hall of *Son of a Smaller Hero,* are both admired and belittled. In one of his essays, written after a year as writer-in-residence at his alma mater, then known as Sir George Williams University, Richler mentions having considered an academic career. What is of additional interest is the informal but polarizing metaphors used in describing the academic and the creative writer: "All of us tend to romanticize the world we nearly chose. In my case, academe, where instead of having to bring home the meat, I would only be obliged to stamp it, rejecting this shoulder of beef as Hank James derivative, or that side of pork as sub-Jimmy Joyce" (*ST*, 17).

Once he was sure that he wanted to write, Richler left college and Canada for Europe. He has mentioned various mixed reasons for this decision made when he was just nineteen years old: he was bored with college; it was the conventional thing to do; Europe offered the promise of adventure and excitement; he felt he could not write in a country culturally barren and innocuous as Canada was then; and he wanted the challenge of proving himself in major literary centers. He spent two years in Europe, living for short periods in Paris, Ibiza, and London. In Paris he joined a circle of aspiring artists (which included Allen Ginsberg, Herbert Gold, Terry Southern, and Mavis Gallant) who had made similar pilgrimages in search of Hemingway's and Henry Miller's Paris. He had his first piece published while living here. A slight short story, "Shades of Darkness: Three Impressions", appeared in *Points,*[9] a Parisian little magazine for young writers.

This story provides the earliest instance of Richler's absorption with ambivalence. As the subtitle indicates, it is really three separate impressions of three different characters (a very obese young Jew, a Jewish-Italian boy living in New York, and a French-Canadian youth) held together tenuously by the author's hesitant tone, which moves between an embarrassing sentimentality and a matter-of-factness conveyed primarily by earthy images and robust colloquialism. Two of the characters experience crucial inner conflicts: the extremely fat man vacillates about killing himself, and the boy of mixed parentage is torn between his Italian and Jewish ancestry. Armand, the French-Canadian, is portrayed as a villain; in fact, he murders through jealousy a Jewish businessman. Richler's attitude to him anticipates his treatment of Duddy Kravitz. Despite Armand's villainy, Richler invites the reader to consider whether he is a victim of his brutal environment which instills in him an instinct for survival.

Richler returned to Canada in 1952 only to leave after one year to take up residence in Europe. When he left Canada the first time, in 1951, he was, like Noah Adler of *Son of a Smaller Hero,* not sure of exactly why, and toward what, he was moving. In 1954, conversely, he appeared less uncertain: the poor Canadian reception of his first novel, *The Acrobats,* and the promise of publication in a literary metropolis seem to point him in one obvious direction. Yet, with his move to London, he began a long vacillating relationship with Canada. He found it necessary to return to Canada and to Montreal in particular sometimes more than twice a year. Though he enjoyed living in England, he was aware of how "schizophrenic some of its delights" were. "You start out, like a model expatriate, hypercritical of your own country but before long you're defending [North] America everywhere."[10] In moving to Britain, he was making a journey to a new life as a man who lives by his pen. He was exposed to better editors and publishers, more prestigious publications, inciting competition, and a more challenging literary climate. His psyche, however, in spite of this new stimulus, remained imbedded in Canada, particularly in the Jewish community of Montreal. All his novels, save *The Acrobats* and *Joshua Then and Now,* were written mainly in England; yet, all his protagonists and the major setting of several of his novels are Canadian, and his thematic concerns, though generally universalized, are examined through Canadian characters, sensibilities, and situations. Richler, like so many writers in exile, discovered that the world he rejected as a suffering individual ironically fed his artistic psyche and imagination.

After much deliberation, he and his family eventually moved back to take up residence in Montreal. The reasons for returning were as mixed and as varied as the reasons for leaving. They involved, as he has mentioned on various occasions,[11] a certain nostalgia for the seasons, the Laurentian Mountains, and hockey; an odd fascination with the Montreal of his childhood; a realization that Canada is no longer a cultural backwater; an acknowledgment that Canada in recent years has been kind to him and has honored him as one of its more prominent writers (though he is aware of the artistic pitfalls of not seeing national prominence in the proper perspective); and a need to return to the wellsprings of his creative imagination. Coming home, however, has not ended his vacillation. Less than a year before leaving England, he told a British journalist he preferred England and that his wife and children would never live anywhere else.[12] He now wants to be able to return often to England: "Eventually I'd like to live in London three or four months of the year . . . I could no more give it up than I could Canada."[13] And though he concedes that Canada is no longer the cultural desert he envisaged it to be as a youth, he is severe in his journalistic assessment, censuring its narrow nationalism, its honoring of mediocrity, and its indiscriminate celebration of

all things Canadian. [14] His novel-in-progress is set in contemporary
Canada; and one published episode, "Manny Moves to Westmount" [15]
(undoubtedly drawn from his recent experience of residing temporarily in the exclusive Westmount area of Montreal), attests, like *Joshua
Then and Now,* his latest novel, to a continuing artistic ambivalence:
a caustic wit commingles with a warm tone in his portrayal of the
Montreal scene.

Even before his first departure for Europe in 1951, Richler was
beginning to develop a fervent interest in journalism. While at
college, he was one of the editors of Sir George Williams weekly
newspaper, the *Georgian,* and he worked part-time with the now de-
funct *Montreal Herald* covering college basketball games and amateur
theatrical nights. Since then he has become a prolific journalist with
well over three hundred pieces in both popular magazines and prestigious journals in Canada, the United States, and England. His cultural and literary articles, general interest pieces, and film and theater
reviews have appeared regularly since the 1950s in publications such
as *New Statesman, Punch, Paris Review, Commentary, Kenyon Review,
Life, Holiday, Maclean's, Tamarack Review, Canadian Literature, Week-
end Magazine,* and *Playboy.* Not unexpectedly for one who has written
so much and in such a range of publications, his journalism is uneven
in quality. Some articles are written simply to startle or to be controversial, some are tediously repetitive and self-plagiarizing, some run
on too long, some are hasty opinions evidently written to be discarded and forgotten, and some are very serious, written with great
deliberation over matter and style. Richler himself has selected and
edited the pieces important to him in four collections: *Hunting Tigers
Under Glass* (1968), *The Street* (1969), *Shovelling Trouble* (1972), and
Notes on an Endangered Species and Others (1974).

Richler takes himself very seriously as a journalist. While he dismisses writing scripts for cinema and television as a means of buying
time for his novels and as a form not for the serious writer, journalism is another matter: "I like journalism," he frankly allows; "I take
as much care of my journalism as anything I write." [16] So committed
is he to this form of writing that he has declared he stands on what
he says in both his journalism and his fiction even though certain
ideas and attitudes in his articles may contradict what appear in his
fiction. [17] This presents a pertinent extension of his artistic ambivalence. The article, "The Holocaust and After," provides a ready illustration. Originally published in 1966 in the *Spectator,* [18] it is an

avowal on Richler's part of blind, indiscriminate hatred of Germans. A tempered version of this essay appeared six years later in *Shovelling Trouble,* yet his uncompromising hatred is still evident from the opening sentence: "The Germans are still an abomination to me" *(ST,* 84). Conversely, in his novels Richler sanctions the response of his protagonists who regret that some Jews are capable of such vindictive hatred. Noah Adler of *Son of a Smaller Hero* finds repugnant the attempts of a Polish victim of Nazi persecution to inculcate in the young Montreal Jews blind atavistic hatred of the Germans. And Jake Hersh of *St. Urbain's Horseman,* who discovers that no matter how much he tries he is incapable of mindless resentment of the Germans, learns to his dismay that the Horseman, his hero, is an incarnation of such brutal, malignant rancor.

The bifocal attitude apparent in the juxtaposition of these journalistic and fictive views of experience is traceable in large measure to the different forms of writing and to the different demands these forms make on the writer. V. S. Naipaul, a contemporary novelist whose experiences and works can be compared profitably with Richler's,[19] made this distinction when he hesitated to accept an offer to write a nonfiction work on the Caribbean: the "novelist works towards conclusions of which he is unaware; and it is better that he should. . . . I felt it as a danger that, having factually analysed the society as far as I was able, I would be unable afterwards to think of it in terms of fiction and that in anything I might write I would be concerned only to prove a point."[20] Richler has no such overt comment on the different creative processes involved in writing journalism and fiction, but a few of his observations hint at an acknowledgment of this difference. Asked in an interview whether he could write a novel on the student revolution of the sixties, he responded: "No. I could possibly write an essay or an article about it but it would be in the nature of an opinion."[21] He has also made a relevant distinction between "commentators," those writers who apparently give opinions mainly, and "documentors," those who mirror the complexities of experience.[22] The distinction Richler and Naipaul have observed argues that nonfiction appraisals generally lack the wider, complex, ironic perceptions of the novel, and that they reflect, in T. S. Eliot's words, "the man who suffers" rather than "the mind which creates."[23] If we accept this distinction, Richler's insistence that he holds steadfast to what he says in both his serious journalism and his fiction—even though they may conflict—reflects an ambivalence deriving from the contradictory responses of the man and the artist, of the active participant and the contemplative creator, of the Horseman and Jake Hersh.

Ambivalent Protagonists

The ambivalent outlook, which Richler's protagonists share with him, is their primary hallmark. The earliest personages, André Bennett of *The Acrobats,* Noah Adler of *Son of a Smaller Hero,* and Norman Price of *A Choice of Enemies,* display the hallmark well. The sensitive and idealistic André is a young artist who undertakes an unfulfilled quest for moral yardsticks in a world bare of any. Early in the book he spells out the importance he and the author attach to the ambivalent vision: the artist must be aware of social injustice, poetic truth, and beauty, André allows, but it is more important "to understand the failings of a man—any man—even as you condemn him."[24] Richler's and André's response to Colonel Kraus, the Nazi war criminal on the run in Spain just after the last war, is one of several illustrations of this credo. Kraus's capacity for mindless cruelty repels both author and protagonist, yet immediately they are aware of his ironically *Jewish* experience of alienation and persecution. André is an Anglo-French Canadian, self-exiled in Spain, and he is the first of many protagonists to reflect another common Richlerian ambivalence: a simultaneous love for and hatred of Canada. His Spanish mistress, who knows him as well as anyone possibly could, perceives that "his anger against his family and his country comes of love" (57). Noah, who believes that his age is a "time of buts and parentheses,"[25] is another sensitive, unanchored, and confused figure searching for himself. He experiences an emotional bind with his Jewish community, rejecting it yet yearning for it. André's and Noah's tormenting feelings—one toward political ideologies in postwar Spain and the other toward Jewish society—kindle in them a sense of futility and ennui which permeates the two novels.

Three years separate *The Acrobats* from *A Choice of Enemies,* wherein Richler, himself twenty-six years old, attempts a study of an ambivalent older character. Norman Price is thirty-eight, almost twice as old as André and Noah. A former university professor, he shows little of his predecessors' romantic, sometimes melodramatic, agonizing, and he is mentally and emotionally more disciplined. Yet he wrestles with intense doubts and conflicts. Political and moral choices plague him. His enervating function as a liaison, with obviously divided allegiance, between two polarized groups of political refugees in Britain (those who fled McCarthy's witch hunt and those who escaped East German communism) underlies his duality of mind. Halfway through the novel his inner conflict becomes so intense, he suffers an attack of temporary amnesia.

In *The Apprenticeship of Duddy Kravitz,* the novel which marks the beginning of Richler's mature period, Richler employs a strong counterpointing of pathos and comedy, satire and compassion, reality and fantasy in his portrayal of the protagonist, toward whom he has openly expressed both admiration and detestation. Richler's ambivalence contributes largely to the scintillating portrait of this young rogue, and it serves to set apart this novel from other less energizingly ambiguous contemporary accounts of the upward struggle of a young urban Jew, such as *What Makes Sammy Run* and *A Stone for Danny Fisher.*[26] Duddy himself has two opposing personalities within him, and he vacillates between his grandfather's morality and his business rivals' corruption.

Unlike *The Apprenticeship of Duddy Kravitz, Cocksure* is intended apparently as satire, yet Richler appears unsure of how to approach the protagonist, particularly midway through the novel. His portrayal of Mortimer Griffin moves back and forth between satire and sympathy—an aspect of the work hinted at by the divergent connotations of the published and the working title, "It's Harder to be Anybody." Mortimer himself is riddled with contradictory desires. He yearns to be part of the ultra-liberal, swinging London set of the 1960s, but his deep moral upbringing constantly foils him. The novel focuses on the follies and vices of the society in which Mortimer finds himself rather than on his inner doubts and mixed feelings. Yet Richler makes us very much aware of them.

St. Urbain's Horseman is a very incisive study of the ambivalent mind. Of Jake Hersh, the protagonist, Richler has stated with uncharacteristic frankness that he "is closer to me than anybody else."[27] At the age of thirty-seven, Jake attempts a self-examination characterized by inner conflicts and contradictory feelings. In his intimate emotional relationships with his wife, his parents, and other relatives and close friends, he experiences strong feelings of attraction and aversion. His experiences as an artist and as a contemporary Jew reflect deep-seated ambivalent feelings as well. A serious film director, he grapples with the artist's desire to be both an active participant and a sedentary observer and recorder of life. A modern Jew, he appreciates the need for Jews to buy off calamity and to temporize, but he still yearns for heroic confrontation and challenge, symbolized by the Horseman in the novel. The protagonist of *Joshua Then and Now*, ten years older than Jake but of a similar temperament, also experiences strong ambivalent feelings. He is both accommodating and sardonic in his treatment of individuals. He is disgusted, for instance, by his vulgarly rich friend, Izzy, yet befriends him. The novel examines the effects of the past on an individual, and Joshua is depicted as simultaneously belittling and yearning for his youthful intensity and idealism.

The ambivalent individual experiences rapidly alternating or simultaneous conflicting feelings or thoughts, but, decidedly, in an extended novel such responses could hardly remain in static equipoise. In Richler's novels the main personages are knowingly or unknowingly searching—futilely—for absolutes which would ease their indecisiveness and irresolution, and the novels are invariably plotted with this spiritual quest in mind. His protagonists initially reject one world for a dubiously better one, then find themselves in a quandary as they struggle to come to grips with the old and the new values to which they now are exposed. Their ambivalence is accentuated by several factors: their inability to convince themselves that what they are escaping is wholly blameworthy, their impotence in defining categorically what they are seeking, and their frustration in determining whether they are in fact escaping or searching.

The use of the alter ego is one of the more concrete ways of expressing polarized thoughts or feelings. Contradictory aspects of the same psyche are embodied separately and distinctly through this device which, like personification, makes abstract qualities and ideas more easily apprehensible. Such use of the alter ego is evident in *St. Urbain's Horseman*. Jake Hersh, who appears to want an undisturbed, sedentary life devoted to his wife and children, is continuously intertwined with the Horseman, Joey Hersh, the embodiment of all that Jake, in his recurring moments of dissatisfaction with his present life, apparently yearns to be: adventurous, heroic, and dedicated to championing just causes. The oneness of these two disparate personalities is insistently displayed through the many instances of mistaken identity, Jake's obsessive search for the Horseman, and their identical initials. A secondary character, the malcontent, Harry Stein, whose pet name, Hershel, is similar to Jake's surname, very likely functions as another alter ego of the protagonist. Jake, who feels fettered by middle-class propriety, at times grudgingly admires, even envies, Stein's vindictive and indecent deeds.

Richler's use of the alter ego is less apparent in the earlier novels, but, reading backwards, one can perceive its germination. The peace-loving André Bennett, for instance, who in the original draft of the novel (among Richler's papers in the University of Calgary Library) is supposed to have killed his lover's father in anger, is linked with the Nazi killer, Kraus. The contemplative Norman Price, as shackled as Jake Hersh by propriety, is a reluctant admirer of Ernst, the self-seeking but freer soul who gives uninhibited expression to his feelings. In discussing Richler's use of the alter ego we must hasten to add that the Richlerian characters who function as such are not devitalized or transparently introduced simply for this purpose. Harry Stein and the Horseman remain vibrant, memorable creations with an existence all their own.

The world in which Richler's protagonists find themselves is one very likely to induce ambivalent reactions, for there are no universal yardsticks of judgment and no clearly indicated rights and wrongs. Traditional and spiritual values are being questioned or have disappeared altogether. Richler's principal personages from André and Noah of the 1940s to Jake and Joshua of the 1970s find themselves in a period of moral and spiritual anarchy. As early as 1956 Richler made this observation which, though simple in its view of history, conveys his assessment of contemporary society: "There has been a collapse of absolute values, whether that value was God or Marx or gold. We are living at a time when superficially life seems meaningless, and we have to make value judgments all the time, it seems, in relation to nothing."[28] Left floundering and groping, Richler's characters are always looking for spiritual mentors. Even one of his most mature protagonists, Jake Hersh, admits his need for a moral editor; and his least conscience-stricken character, Duddy Kravitz, whether he is conscious of it or not, looks for spiritual guidance from his high-minded grandfather in an amoral business world.

Structure

By his own admission, Richler has difficulty structuring his novels.[29] They tend to be more episodic and mechanical than organically flowing. Scenes and incidents are sometimes introduced for their own

sake rather than as digested and cohesive portions of the novel. It is
not difficult to see how Richler's ambivalent vision encourages this
episodic structuring, particularly in *The Apprenticeship of Duddy Kravitz* where the author's mixed feelings toward his protagonist are most
cogently illustrated. Richler's repulsion and admiration unfold
through the structural technique of antithetically alternating, almost
in clockwork fashion, incidents or a series of incidents in which
Duddy is favorably presented with those in which he is a scoundrel.
The Acrobats is, in the main, a series of set scenes (featuring labored
conversations on the contrasting ideologies to which André is exposed) loosely strung together by a thin *ménage à trois* plot. Alternating episodes dealing with Norman Price's experiences, here with the
American émigrés who fled McCarthy's witch hunt, and there with
East German refugees, largely dictate the structure of *A Choice of
Enemies*, which, like the earlier novel, makes use of a thin triangular
love affair to hold the episodes together. In *Son of a Smaller Hero*,
Noah Adler's present wanderings in the non-Jewish world are continuously juxtaposed with his current and recalled experiences of his
Jewish community. And *St. Urbain's Horseman*, possibly Richler's
most complexly structured novel, employs involved flashbacks within
flashbacks and several interwoven narrative threads. Nevertheless,
perceivable as a dominant structural device is the juxtaposing and the
alternating of scenes indicative of the protagonist's mixed feelings. In
fact, it is in this novel, patently a study of an ambivalent mind, that
within single scenes sudden shifts occur from one conflicting mood to
another, and abrupt, self-contradictory or neutralizing phrases appear
such as "But - but -" and "And yet - and yet -."

Tone

In providing the individual the opportunity of seeing both sides of
an issue, the ambivalent vision encourages him to have the second
thought, or to turn a more accommodating eye on human experience,
or at least to hesitate to condemn out of hand human shortcomings
and frailties. Such responses militate against cogent satire. The satirical vision springs from firm convictions of what is right and wrong,
unimbued with any hesitancy, vacillation, or irresolution. The satirist
in the published form of his work does not weigh, balance, and sift
evidence, resolve queries, wrestle with doubts like a member of the
judicial bench; he more closely approximates the prosecutor, who,

having convinced himself of the accused's guilt, sets about relentlessly to convict him. Richler's binary vision allows him an explanation of the thing satirized; he is able to probe beyond the moment of absurdity and vice to the extenuating circumstances. He most assuredly has a talent for satirical scenes. *The Incomparable Atuk, Cocksure,* and scattered satirical pieces in almost every novel are clear evidence of this. Yet, even in the novels consciously intended as satire, his ambivalence tends to mollify stringent satire to such an extent that one wonders whether the predominant vision in those particular novels can indeed be categorically described as satirical. In *Cocksure,* the Star Maker—significantly a secondary character—is a satirical grotesque, and he and his followers are obviously mocked and ridiculed. The major part of the novel, however, is about Mortimer Griffin's social and professional activities, and whatever satire is directed against the often feckless Mortimer is considerably softened by Richler's invitation to peer at the extenuating circumstances. In fact, the author's dual attitude makes it possible for the reader to see this novel more as a study of the pathetic little man than as a sustained satire on society. In most of Richler's novels satire occurs in scattered scenes as a minor tone, and it is either tempered by the presence of irresolute protagonists or given in set pieces usually at odds with the rest of the novel.

Richler's involvement with film and television provides another dimension to his ambivalent tone and attitude. Time and again he rejects scriptwriting as unworthy of the talents of truly dedicated novelists. "Like most novelists," he declares, "I am conditioned to working for months on material I discuss with nobody, because to talk about it is to risk losing it."[30] He considers making films, on the other hand, to be a group activity involving various technicians among whom the most lowly and expendable is the writer who adapts thrillers and best sellers. Even those who adapt serious novels or write serious original screenplays are robbed of artistic independence and satisfaction; in the case of the adapter, the work remains essentially the original novelist's, and no matter what positive contribution the writer of the original screenplay makes, film making, says Richler on the authority of the movie director, Federico Fellini, "belongs more than anything to the writer-director."[31]

Though Richler would have us believe that as a rule he approaches scriptwriting with little fervor, and that his sporadic participation is primarily to buy time for his true vocation of writing novels, his actual relationship with the form is not all that simple or straightfor ward. A child of the age when the screen was a popular cultural force in North America, Richler recalls its powerful influence on himself: "You were brought up on film, and so you've absorbed that before you even thought of being a writer."[32] He nostalgically remembers cutting morning classes to attend the cinema. His memoirs and essays often and fondly name films and movie stars of his youth and refer to memorable dramatic or comic moments in particular films. In later years Richler was enticed into the cinematic world as a scriptwriter. He wrote and adapted many popular as well as more serious scripts for Canadian and British television and for the cinema. He is credited, for instance, with adapting for the screen John Braine's *Life at the Top* and Wilfred Fienburgh's *No Love for Johnnie* (a study of a self-centered, ambitious rogue, to all appearances an older and British version of Duddy Kravitz). Richler evidently has a facility in this form of writing, and his services are always in demand. But his reiterated aversion to the hack work involved and his preference for concentrating on his novels make him reject most offers unless economic needs pressure him into compromise.

Countering this aversion, however, are his undeniable attraction to the form and his fascination with its ambiance. His own unambiguous comments in his essays and memoirs illustrate this. In "Why I Write" Richler the novelist, who functions best in isolation, admits he is not reluctant to be acquainted with directors and stars, and to "skitter on the periphery of festooned circles, know plenty of inside stories" (*ST,* 15). Evidence is also there in the numerous occasions, major and minor, when the setting, the characters, and the themes of his fiction involve the film world. *St. Urbain's Horseman* has a film director as its protagonist, and one of its memorable inset scenes is a baseball game replete with the intrigues and complex relationships of the film world's personnel; *A Choice of Enemies* examines the plight of Hollywood refugees of McCarthyism in London; *Joshua Then and Now* has an extended account of Joshua's trip to Hollywood in which Richler shows how writers are at the mercy of insensitive film makers; *Cocksure* reverberates with sardonic accounts of mindless stars and manipulating producers, and it has a fine study of a moonstruck waif of celluloid whose world is a make-believe silver screen with dissolves and happy endings; even Duddy Kravitz is enthralled by films and starts his own film company with a pseudo ex-Hollywood director. In all his novels, Richler shows a preference for dramatic scenes—almost always consummately done—over narrative description, and he frequently uses other cinematic techniques and forms: the fast-paced external narrative; the externalizing of emotions in physical action and setting; the inset movie script, sometimes only peripherally involved with the central theme and plot; the montage, the dissolves, and quick time changes.

Several of Richler's original scripts and adaptations for television and the cinema were intended for the popular and commercial market and were relative successes as such. Richler the scriptwriter is certainly not unaware of how to use suspense, sex, fast-paced narrative, shocking language, and arresting and faddish themes to attract and hold the general audience. Entertainment and popularity are inbred in the film world. At a reasonable cultural level Richler is not averse to these attributes, and their manifestations to varying degrees in the conception and realization of his novels are undeniable, even though he has observed that "any serious writer is a moralist and only incidentally an entertainer" (*ST*, 20). In conflict with Richler the serious novelist is the entertainer who seeks the best-seller list, who agreed to the more alluring title of *Cocksure*, and who admittedly looks at most reviews basically as market reports, noting which will restrict or encourage sales of his books (*ST*, 16). One must hasten to add that there is nothing incompatible in being a serious and popular writer. Joseph Conrad accomplished this without compromising himself. One should also add that Richler never really sacrifices the serious spheres of his work for the sake of rank popularity and entertainment. What happens is that in his better works his desire both to entertain and to be serious—two requirements Richler considers antithetical—produces an absorbing tension of purpose in his novels.

A fine example of this is the sordid rape trial with which *St. Urbain's Horseman* begins and ends. This narrative is evidently used as a framework within which Richler copes structurally with the novel's bulging array of characters, situations, and experiences. But employing this particular narrative is surely intended as an enticement to the reader. Significantly, however, Richler does not allow his account of the trial to degenerate into a sensational tabloid report. Some of the more effective dramatic scenes are set in the Old Bailey; and for these, Richler did extensive and serious research, observing and interviewing for months legal, judicial, and investigative experts. But a stronger justification for this seductive structural narrative is its subtle thematic implication: Jake's alleged rape of the German maid, whose father was a Nazi dentist and who eventually victimizes Jake, is an integral part of the novel's ambitious attempt to create a mythology for the contemporary Jew. Richler's mixed desire in this novel to write an entertaining work as well as a serious study of experience provides an attractive commingling of lusty diversion and of profundity, an underlying aspect of his maturing style. *Cocksure* also illustrates this. Its coarse language and shocking sexual scenes, and particularly its published title, seem deliberately intended to seek the notoriety the novel did achieve (it was banned in Australia and in W. H. Smith bookstores in England). But beneath its apparent sensational bawdiness is a serious purpose. Richler himself has emphasized that this is "a *very* moral book";[33] and Leslie Fiedler underlines the novelist's ambivalence when, though he perceives in Richler an affinity for "the atrocious—the dirty joke turned somehow horrific," he describes the novel as a "middlebrow satire . . . however deliciously gross, an anti-genteel defence of the genteel tradition."[34]

Chapter Two

The Montreal Novels:
Son of a Smaller Hero
and *The Apprenticeship*
of Duddy Kravitz

Referring to the Montreal Jewish community of the 1940s and 1950s, Richler has observed: "That was my time, my place, and I have elected myself to get it right."[1] Richler re-creates this time and place in *Son of a Smaller Hero* and *The Apprenticeship of Duddy Kravitz* so evocatively that Desmond Pacey was persuaded to say he succeeds in bringing "his native city of Montreal . . . to life as no writer has been able to do before."[2] But Richler's achievement in these novels—the only ones set almost exclusively in Montreal—is more than just a vivid portrayal of setting. He provides incisive studies of two complex characters, one a tormented artist, Noah Adler, and the other a young scoundrel, Duddy Kravitz. Moreover, both novels have a strong authorial mediating presence characterized by an ambivalent outlook toward the Montreal Jewish community; this creates within the works a remarkable tension and an energizing ambiguity, but also has encouraged inadvertently antithetical assessments of the author's attitude and tone as that of either a harsh satirist or a quaint sentimentalist.[3] Though these novels focus on the Jewish community, Richler is not preoccupied with ethnic issues. He looks beneath the racial to the human and, like Bernard Malamud, uses the Jewish world as a metaphor for human experience. Despite his vivid evocation of the Montreal Jewish community of his youth in these novels, Richler is not simply attempting sociohistorical treatises. *Son of a Smaller Hero* and *The Apprenticeship of Duddy Kravitz* transcend time, place, and race, and become novels that are at once Jewish, Canadian, and universal.

Son of a Smaller Hero

Son of a Smaller Hero (1955) is Richler's second novel, but it pre-
cedes *The Acrobats* (1954) in the chronology of the author's own experience, for while *The Acrobats* derives from his exile as a young man
in Europe, *Son of a Smaller Hero* grows out of the earlier years in the
Montreal Jewish ghetto. The many evident parallels in this novel between his protagonist's and his own life obliged Richler to include a
prefatory note disclaiming any autobiographical intention. This, of
course, must be heeded, for however much Richler draws on his own
life in this novel, it is a work of the imagination and must be considered as such. The author has some difficulty, however, keeping
himself consistently apart from his creation, and though the book is
written in the third person, it often seems to be told from Noah's
point of view whether he is in the scene or not. The absence of aesthetic distance between himself and his protagonist weakens Richler's
otherwise perceptive study of Noah, for he appears occasionally to
share Noah's youthful posturing and his assumption of moral superi-
ority to almost everyone, as in the scene where Noah meets the Gol-
denbergs at their Ste. Agathe retreat. This lack of objectivity
becomes more readily apparent if *Son of a Smaller Hero* is compared
with a later work like *St. Urbain's Horseman* where a mature Richler
succeeds in sustaining an objective appraisal of the protagonist whose
experiences quite often parallel his.

Richler's primary concern in *Son of a Smaller Hero* is his exploration
of Noah's inner conflicts and contradictions, but this does not prevent
him from relating a characteristically absorbing narrative. He takes
the thin and familiar story of a rebellious youth leaving home and
imbues it with a freshness and vitality by vividly evoking the Montreal setting, by introducing many well-drawn secondary characters,
by interweaving several minor plots, and by carefully managing suspense. A second-generation Canadian from an orthodox Jewish home,
Noah wants to leave his family to be on his own because of the constant bickering between his feckless father, Wolf, and his over-
ambitious mother, Leah, and because of the tyrannical ways of his
grandfather, Melech, who rules his extended family with an iron
hand. Living on his own, however, complicates rather than explicates
his life, for while working as a taxi driver and attending evening
classes at Wellington College, he meets Professor Theo Hall, a gentile who, perceiving Noah's love of literature, takes an interest in him

and offers him accommodation in his home. Eventually, Noah becomes intimately involved with the professor's wife, Miriam, who leaves her husband to live with Noah. During this period, he drifts marginally between his former and his present communities.

Noah abandons Miriam soon after his father dies while trying to save a box belonging to Melech in a fire set by Melech's youngest son, Shloime. Wolf becomes a martyr because the public believes he tried to save the sacred scrolls found in the box when in actuality, as Melech and Noah know, he really believed the box contained money. Noah discovers that his grandfather preserves in this box also a snapshot of a Polish girl and some love letters he wrote to her but never mailed. She evidently was someone Melech as a young man in Europe loved but, inflexibly heeding tradition, he felt he could not marry her since she was a gentile. The unmailed letters show that he still yearns for her. After the death of his father, Noah tries to accommodate himself to the Adler extended family, which is now dominated by the affluent Uncle Max. But this nouveau-riche environment, Max's attempt to exploit Wolf's apparent martyrdom, and the emotional demands of his own possessive mother begin to oppress him, so he escapes once again, this time to Europe. Richler adds to the complexity of this plot by including several peripherally related accounts of incidents involving a wide range of minor characters. There are, for instance, the betrothal of Melech's youngest daughter to a sensual youth, Shloime's robbery of Panofsky's shop, Panofsky's relationship with his sons, Miriam's with her impoverished father, and Theo's with his overprotective mother.

Son of a Smaller Hero offers the most graphic description of the Montreal Jewish ghetto during the 1940s and 1950s that is to be found in Richler's novels. The author's senses are particularly accurate in this book when he describes the sights, sounds, and smells of everyday life in homes, streets, parks, shops, taverns, and work places. As a rule he evokes this environment unobtrusively in dramatic scenes, but so intent is he on re-creating it as accurately as possible that he often resorts to long, incredibly detailed descriptive passages and occasional undisguised authorial discourses on ghetto life. The absorption with authenticity of setting should in no way be construed as an unseemly indulgence in the exotic or as a simple sociohistorical interest in Jewish ghetto life per se. Richler's main consideration in this novel is his sensitive protagonist's complex relationship with his environment, and since this is the world *within* which and *against* which he struggles, it is of necessity inclusively portrayed.

In his study of Noah's complicated involvement with his Jewish community Richler concentrates on two related problems. The first is Noah's tormenting ambivalent attitude toward his environment, and the other is his nascent awareness that though he resents his grandfather's severe morality, he himself ironically is equally severe in his judgment of others. His love-hate relationship with his community remains fairly constant throughout the novel, but he does develop away from his grandfather's absolutism and inflexibility and gradually becomes more tolerant. The book captures well the anguish he experiences when caught between his acceptance and rejection of his family, and between his tendency to judge others sharply and his desire to be more understanding than his uncompromising grandfather.

Noah's ambivalence is felt throughout the novel, from the first chapter where he escapes from yet yearns for his community to the last where he tells his grandfather "I am going and I'm not going."[4] His emotional bind is poignantly evoked in the opening scene where he is shown adjusting himself to his apartment. It is immediately clear that instead of feeling emancipated on having left his stifling home, he is overcome by loneliness and appears to have lost whatever firm inner directives prompted him to live on his own. He has little rapport with the people he first meets in his new world. A drunk who makes love to a girl in the back seat of his taxi angers him, and he finds it hard to hide his disdain for his landlady who presumes he is a medical student because he has a copy of *The Naked and the Dead* among his belongings. Reviewing his depressing first day of freedom, he reflexively recalls his family and friends. Such moments of recollection given in the form of flashbacks are evidently Richler's method of introducing the reader to the pre-history of the novel, but, juxtaposed as they are with Noah's contrasting current experiences, they serve also as a recurring structural indicator of his binary feelings and responses. Wondering about his mother, "lonely in her kitchen chair, lonely even in a crowded streetcar," he reviews his decision to leave home and is no longer categorically sure he has done the right thing: *"It is necessary, at times, to hurt others. But I'm hurting her very much. I'd better be right"* (26). The world from which he escapes, viewed from his empty lodging, appears anachronistic but rich in warmth and humor, and he comes to realize that though the Adlers live in a cage, "that cage, with all its faults, had justice and safety and a kind of felicity" (36).

This flashback to his family life is followed immediately by another that shows his ambivalent response not just to his family but to his Jewish community as a whole. A Polish Jew who had experienced the horror of Nazi persecution was lecturing a group of teen-agers, among whom were Noah and his friends, on the need for solidarity among Jews. Though Noah sympathized with his suffering at the hands of the Nazis, he realized that the man was encouraging atavistic hatred in the youthful audience, and he struggled against being as mesmerized by him as were his friends. After the lecture, the speaker invited the youths to join hands in a traditional folk dance. Noah's response to this invitation reflects his mixed emotions. Initially he stood apart watching his friends join hands and form an exclusive circle for the dance, but, feeling sharp pricks of conscience, he attempted to break into the ring of dancers but "they were whirling past too fast, and he was spun back and away from them defiantly, like a counterfeit coin from a cashier" (28). The image of the counterfeit coin effectively points up Noah's conflicting feelings: he knew he could not share the prejudice of his friends, yet he saw himself as a fraud for not doing so.

Noah's dissatisfaction with his community has much to do with its rigid customs and inherited biases which he feels create a garrison mentality. As his artistic sensibility germinates, he begins also to judge his environment by aesthetic standards, and this further complicates his response. As a boy he once spied on gentiles at a restricted beach near his Jewish summer camp and was repelled by their ugly prejudice against Jews; but he also was impressed by the beauty of the people and the place, which induced him to make unfavorable comparisons with his own squalid camp. Later, as a college freshman, he discovered beauty in music and blamed the belatedness of his discovery on his community's fears and resentments:

The first time Noah had been to a concert the orchestra had played *The Four Seasons* of Vivaldi and he had been so struck by it that he had felt something like pain. He had not suspected that men were capable of such beauty. He had been startled. So he had walked out wandering into the night, not knowing what to make of his discovery. All those stale lies that he had inherited from others, all those cautionary tales, and those other dreadful

things, facts, that he collected like his father did stamps, knowledge, all
that passed away, rejected, dwarfed by the entry of beauty into his consciousness. (73–74)

The basic intensity of the novel springs from Richler's penetrating
study of Noah's ambivalent relationship with three sets of people: his
parents, Miriam and Theo, and, most crucial of all, his grandfather.
The bitterness between his parents, victims of an arranged marriage,
is certainly a factor in Noah's decision to live on his own. He is suffocated by their constant quarreling, by his father's inanity and daw-
dling, and by his possessive mother who charts ambitious courses for
him and seeks to set him against his father. Yet Noah shows an underlying regret for their wasted lives. He is very conscious of his father's sterile existence. A simple, unpretentious, passive little man,
Wolf takes pleasure in practical jokes and obscene puns, and spends
his spare time in the cinema, playing pinochle, and recording all the
trivial facts of his empty life in his diary written in a simplistic code
of his own invention. In the only extended meeting between father
and son Noah shows an aching solicitude for his father's sad lot: "He
found him sitting at his desk in the den. Wolf nodded and wiggled
his ears and made his glasses go up and down on his nose. I'm your
son, Noah thought. Do you count me among your tormentors too?"
(121).
    Noah's love-hate relationship with his mother is explicitly ac-
knowledged by him. "Alternately," he observes, "he felt strong attraction then revulsion for her" (95). In contrast to her husband, Leah
is ambitious, pretentious, and, coming from the cultured home of a
scribe, contemptuous of her husband whom she considers coarse and
common. The only time she reaps any benefit from her marriage is
after Wolf's death when she delights in the role of being the widow
of an apparent hero—though she sheds no tears for him. Noah resents
her at times, yet he tries to be patient with her, perceiving that to
escape the disappointments of the real world she lives a suspended life
hoping to achieve fulfillment through him. He accommodates—up to
a point—this possessive attitude toward him. At the end of the
novel, when he feels he must leave her and his community, he shows
some genuine filial concern though he suspects she uses her illness to
keep him with her.
    As Miriam gradually becomes more dependent on and more pos-
sessive of Noah, his affair with her begins "to duplicate" (124) his

love-hate relationship with his mother. In spite of the space allotted it, this affair is never incisively examined. Richler emphasizes Miriam's function less as a lover and more as a representative of her community and as a foil to Noah. She serves as a means of exposing Noah to an alternative world which, when he discovers it has "as little veracity, if more novelty" (106) than his own, both intensifies and lessens his confusion and sense of being adrift. The prolonged account of the love affair enables Richler to create this new society—against which and within which Noah temporarily struggles—almost as graphically as the Jewish environment. As a foil to Noah, Miriam (whose name in Hebrew means *rebellion*) is portrayed repudiating completely and unequivocally her early life of poverty with a derelict father of whom she is ashamed. She searches in vain for a sense of belonging in bohemian circles. Her life with Theo has become barren and she now turns to Noah in whom she sees a kindred spirit. But while Noah, true to his biblical name, appears to survive his environment at the end of the novel, she becomes a pathetic victim of hers.

Richler's uneven style in his portrayal of the Noah-Miriam affair further prevents their complicated relationship from being effectively realized. Stilted dialogue, overwriting, and melodramatic scenes, such as Theo's literally catching Noah with his pants down in Miriam's bedroom, too often counterbalance bracing and genuine writing. The derivative style Richler uses at certain points to heighten his protagonist's feelings conveys an emotional speciousness. At one moment, Noah is depicted unabashedly drawing from John Donne: "Let it be said of us that we made no plans. That the others schemed, got money and position, honours, futures, but that we—who dissented ruined ourselves with loving" (104); at another, Richler invokes D. H. Lawrence's sensual reveling in the natural world:

> The hills greyed and black clouds swirled, lightning cracked and then the rumbling distant, closer, and the rushing in the trees. Down, down, swoosh after swoosh of rain. Eventually he kicked off his shoes and, up again, wandered into the woods singing the prayers of his boyhood boldly. At last the rain stopped. Clouds broke up and softened until the sun—magnanimous beyond compare—condescended to shine down in the woods and on the reappearing hills, as if nothing, nothing at all, had ever happened. (117–18)

Miriam herself lacks authenticity—an observation Richler, who admits difficulty in portraying female characters,[5] is not likely to con-

tradict. Her early life is written about more confidently, perhaps
because her background of poverty echoes the Jewish ghetto, but
more likely because she is portrayed sexlessly as a child rather than as
a girl. The last glimpse of Miriam in the novel is at a New Year's
party where her perturbed mother-in-law times how long she stays
with her lover in a locked bedroom. The narrator of this scene is not
indicated clearly; he could be either the omniscient author or an absent Noah. Consequently, it is difficult to know exactly how it
should be taken: it could be a pathetic confirmation of Noah's aban-
donment of Miriam; it could also be an instance of Richler's inability
to resist an appealing comic scene even if it is tonally inconsistent.

Noah both admires and ridicules Miriam's husband. His relationship with Theo, however, lacks psychological plausibility primarily
because of a serious ambiguity in Richler's depiction of this English
professor. Richler both romanticizes and satirizes him. V. S. Pritchett points out an inherent difficulty that writers often face when portraying characters outside their own ethnic, national, or class groups:
"It is normal to fail with foreigners: Dickens caricatured the French,
Kipling the Indians, George Eliot romanticized the Jews. Class also
has its foreignness: Lawrence was bad about baronets, Hardy was lus-
cious about Society. . . . The danger really is that in writing about
the alien thing the novelist will fall back on a blatant or hopefully
disguised convention."[6] Richler's portrayal of Theo and other gentile
characters, even in his later novels (such as Calder in *The Apprenticeship of Duddy Kravitz* and Ormsby-Fletcher in *St. Urbain's Horseman*),
reveals this problem. Compared to the Jewish characters, Theo, when
not satirized, is stereotyped and devitalized in scenes dealing with the
triangular love affair. As a butt now and again for Richler's satire on
barren academic figures, however, he is more effective since satirical
portraits are concerned restrictively with the individual's shortcomings rather than with his whole personality.

Noah's relationship with his grandfather, characterized by very
strong ambivalent feelings in both, is far more significant to the main
issues of the novel than his relationship with Miriam despite the
extended treatment this love affair receives. Noah admires his grandfather's sense of responsibility to his family but resents his unswerving
adherence to harsh religious laws and his stern, just, and merciless
God. Melech regards his sensitive grandson highly and favors him
more than his own children, but is angered by his rejection of the
traditional way of life. Richler focuses on two pivotal incidents in

Noah's relationship with his grandfather. The first, which occurred when Noah was just eleven, initiated the ambivalent feelings each has for the other. On a visit to his grandfather's coal yard, young Noah had observed the employees cheating customers at the scales and reported this to his grandfather who was chatting with a gentile customer. Melech, familiar with what went on in his coal yard, tried to ignore Noah, who, believing his grandfather had not heard him, started to repeat what he had seen, and was slapped into silence by Melech. Immediately Melech regretted his action and chased after Noah who was fleeing from him. Here is a potential illustration of the pejorative myth of the usurious Jew which Richler presumably could have presented as such but does not. What concerns him is the pathos of the subsequent strained relationship of two characters who once were devoted to each other, and the irony of the old man's inability to understand Noah's morality and to make Noah understand his. Melech constantly recalls the incident, and though he acknowledges his grandson's uprightness, he would like him to realize that his cheating at the scales is no more than a trick of the trade which counters his customers' own wily actions. In slapping his grandson to forestall his accusation, he was protecting him from the gentile customer who would jump at an opportunity to make derogatory comments against Jews. The older Noah eventually comes to accept without censure that his grandfather saw nothing wrong with his underhanded business method and is aware that, despite this incident, so strong is Melech's morality that he would be brokenhearted if he were told of his youngest son's participation in the violent robbery at Panofsky's. However, though Noah understands this, he wants to be unfettered to make his own choices and commitments which his grandfather's rigidity denies him.

The second incident, Noah's perusal of the contents of Melech's box, is most crucial to Noah's search for himself. Within this box Noah discovers the picture of Helga, the young gentile whom his grandfather loved years ago in Europe. Melech's strict adherence to ethnic law prevented him from marrying her. His constant daydreaming of Helga, the souvenirs he preserves of her, and the letters he still writes to her without mailing, all belie his belief that he did the right thing in not marrying her, and that he is a better and stronger man than his grandson for his steadfast adherence to ethnic tradition. Noah's discovery of this hidden part of his grandfather's life leads him to realize the difference between Melech's values and his own, and takes him a step closer to an understanding of himself. Noah comes to accept what Melech will never allow, that compromise is possible without betrayal, and that tolerance and flexibility supersede unthinking adherence to harsh laws. Melech's youngest son once accused Noah of being no less severe and uncompromising than his grandfather, but in Noah's last meeting with Melech he happily realizes that Shloime's analysis of him is far from true, for "Melech, in Noah's place, would have told his grandfather that his youngest son had started the fire. Melech, in his place, would have had God and would have done what was just" (203). Though Noah is possibly right in making this distinction between himself and Melech, he finds it difficult to put his philosophy into practice consistently, and the final pages depict him still veering between censure and tolerance.

Noah's distressful relation with his community and his painful search for himself impart to the novel a pervasively sombre mood which is reinforced by the recurring imagery of oppressive heat and bitter cold, of garbage heaps, and particularly of blackness. These images, given early in the first chapter and reinforced again and again in later chapters, create a dismal impression which stays with the reader throughout the novel:

The street reeks of garlic and quarrels and bill collectors: orange crates, stuffed full with garbage and decaying fruit, are piled slipshod in most alleys. Swift children gobble pilfered plums, slower cats prowl the fish market. After the water truck has passed, the odd dead rat can be seen floating down the gutter followed fast by rotten apples, cigar butts, chunks of horse manure, and a terrifying zigzag of flies. . . . After the rains there was always the heat again. The flies returned, the old men retreated to their beds, and all the missing odours of the heat reappeared with a new intensity. (15–16)

The few pleasant days mentioned serve but to emphasize by contrast unhappy experiences. Melech, for instance, is portrayed reading the obituary column on a spring day, and Wolf's funeral takes place on "a bright morning" (143) in summer. Blackness is emphasized in Melech's coal yard, in Wolf's home, in Leah's dreams, and in bleak streets. Noah himself often wanders in the dark night and looks at the dark sky. The metaphorical use of light-dark images is common. Melech and Leah, no longer close to Noah, feel he could have been *"the brightness"* (19) of their lives, and during his brief period of hap-

piness with Miriam, Noah observes that the "darkness around us
. . . belongs to others" (102).

Though the action of the novel extends just over a year when Noah
is twenty years old, it is still possible to consider *Son of a Smaller Hero*
on one level as a *bildungsroman,* for the reader is able to observe
Noah's development as an artist. Several flashbacks to Noah's childhood tell of his appreciation of literature, of his awakening to beauty,
and of his traumatic but enlightening experiences with racial prejudices and religious absolutes. The chronological arrangement of
Noah's current experiences which conveys a causal sequence of events
and the temporal titles given to the five parts of the novel—Summer
1952, Autumn and Winter 1952, Spring 1953, Summer 1953, and
Autumn and Winter 1953–4—point up the theme of maturation, as
does the conspicuous frequency of phrases marking the passage of
years, seasons, and even weeks, days, and hours: "On that Sunday
morning in the summer of 1952" (17), "Noah . . . looked at his
watch. 5.15" (25), "The next morning, Friday" (61), "Those first
two weeks" (114).

A symmetrical arrangement of the first and the last scenes of the
novel—a structural component which is organically integrated with
the well-defined chronological organization of *Son of a Smaller Hero*—
further alerts the reader both to Noah's growth and to his ambivalence. The book begins and ends with Noah leaving home. Each
departure is associated with a Sunday family gathering and with a
meeting of Noah and his grandfather. Both Sunday gatherings are introduced with a similar phrase: "On that Sunday morning in the
summer of 1952, as under a stern sun. . . . " (17), and "On that
first Sunday of the winter of 1954, as under a stern sun . . . " (195).
Both meetings of grandfather and grandson begin with the same
phrasing—"Noah, who at that moment was parked across the
street . . . " (36, 201)—and express sentiments that are worded in
the same way: "The Adlers lived in a cage and that cage, with all its
faults, had justice and safety and a kind of felicity" (36, 201). There
are significant differences, however, between these initial and concluding scenes. In the first gathering, Melech is a dominant figure;
in the last, he is relegated to a corner armchair as Max takes over as
head of the family. Noah's first meeting with Melech is characterized
by violent anger and bitterness; the last meeting concludes on a note
of reconciliation. When Noah leaves home in the first part, he is be-

wildered and lost; in the last chapter, he has a better sense of direction. The symmetrical pattern is evident also in the second, third, and fourth parts. The third tells of Wolf's death and constitutes the climax of the novel. The two preceding parts relate Noah's attraction to the gentile world of Miriam and Theo though he is still emotionally tied to his Jewish community; the succeeding parts contrastingly tell of his disenchantment with the gentile society which nevertheless beckons him.

The major portion of the novel is narrated through Noah's consciousness, and since most of the adverse comments against the Montreal Jewish society are essentially the response of a troubled, ambivalent protagonist, they tend to be more demonstrative of Noah's character than of any cogent satirical intention on Richler's part. Richler is more preoccupied with exploring Noah's mixed feelings, his piques, his frustrations, his moodiness, his anxieties, and his drunken rages than with employing him as a satirical persona. There are occasions, however, when Richler is unquestionably speaking directly and omnisciently, and these scattered scenes are early attestations to the satirical vein in his writings that is so often at odds with his counterpointing tolerance.

The first instance of this authorial voice is found in the set piece on the Montreal Jewish ghetto in the opening chapter. Though the observations in this passage are intended as Noah's, they patently constitute an authorial discourse punctuated with satirical censure of the self-centered, status-conscious parvenu. The young novelist barely manages to refine his overpowering resentment of these figures into satire. Of such censure of the middle-class Jew, Richler has said: "One of the things I was most concerned with in *Son of a Smaller Hero* was that it seems to me that class loyalties in Montreal were much stronger than so-called Jewish loyalties and traditions; that the middle-class Jew has much more in common with the middle-class Gentile than he has with the Jew who works for him in his factory."[7] In this set satirical passage, as in others, Richler's criticism quite clearly is directed against not ethnic, but common, human shortcomings.

Richler interrupts Noah's point of view again in two crowd scenes. In one, he satirizes the coarse and insensitive figures assembled at the site of the recovery of Wolf's charred body. Commenting on the crowd's need for melodrama to ease the boredom of their lives on the hot summer day, Noah tells Miriam: "We could charge half a buck a head. But they don't mean bad" (138). The antithesis in his comment attests to Noah's efforts to be tolerant of the ghetto people; however, the controlling voice here is not Noah's but the author's whose firm satirical tone informs the passage.

The account of the funeral service for Wolf, the other crowd scene, in which Richler experiments with multiple points of view, has several sharp satirical portraits of the lesser mourners, such as the literary hack who "wrote speeches that were read by philanthropic millionaires at Zionist banquets" (143) and the rabbi who "believed in God as an insurance salesman believes in Prudential" (151). The personages satirized in these two crowd scenes have no thematic or narrative function in the novel. They perhaps add somewhat to the authenticity of setting. Primarily they are introduced to serve Richler's satirical impulse which at times he appears unable to subdue even if it occasions in his novel long digressions and inconsistency of tone—as is most clearly shown in the funeral scene where Noah's deep feelings are jarringly juxtaposed with the author's satirical voice.

Son of a Smaller Hero, written by Richler when he was just twenty-four, must be read as an apprenticeship work. There are some obvious weaknesses: the author does not always stand apart from his protagonist and disengage himself from his occasional righteous anger and self-regarding attitude; satiric distortion at times interrupts impressively graphic evocation of Montreal; melodrama interferes here and there with scenes of felt experience; certain episodes tend to have a disproportionate emphasis; and the theme of self-discovery is not always kept in sharp focus. Yet the novel impresses with its brilliant setting, its gallery of honestly perceived and depicted characters, its richness of absorbing situations and episodes, its intensity of tone, and its remarkably perceptive portrait of a sensitive protagonist striving to know himself.

The Apprenticeship of Duddy Kravitz

To come fresh from Richler's first three novels to *The Apprenticeship of Duddy Kravitz* is to be made quickly aware of why most critics consider this, his fourth novel, to be the best of his early works and one of his finest novels. An unprecedented assurance and confidence here mark a new stage in his writing. The narrative pace is livelier. The dialogue and dramatic scenes are more skillfully presented. Humor becomes organic and integrated and is not simply relegated to set passages. And Richler's ambivalence toward his protagonist, more perceptible here than in the previous works, imparts a vitalizing tension and an enriching complexity.

The main narrative is, like that of *Son of a Smaller Hero*, a commonplace: the novel traces the progress of a fledgling entrepreneur from poverty to relative wealth and recognition. The protagonist, Duddy Kravitz, lives in the impoverished St. Urbain Street area of Montreal of the 1940s. Almost everyone including his father, Max, and his brother, Lennie, consider him a social and academic nonentity with no future. His childhood and schooldays are briefly recounted but with enough details to show him to be mischievous, crooked, and prematurely worldly wise. Richler stresses one particular incident during this period which haunts Duddy throughout the novel: a prank call by him to his teacher, MacPherson, indirectly brings about the death of MacPherson's ailing wife. Only Duddy's grandfather pays him any attention during his boyhood, and he inadvertently fires Duddy's ambition to seek out and acquire land by telling him that "a man without land is nobody."[8]

The major portion of the novel focuses on the period of just over a year after Duddy's graduation from high school when he sets about with tremendous zest and drive to buy up all the land around Lac St. Pierre, a beautiful area he discovers in the Laurentians with potential for a vast holiday resort. No principles or scruples obstruct him in his relentless pursuit of this property. He cheats, lies, exploits, and blackmails. However, another side of him is revealed in his sympathetic concern for members of his family. He seeks to comfort his dying Uncle Benjy by fetching home his wife, and he averts his brother's expulsion from medical school for performing an illegal abortion. At the end of the novel, Duddy acquires his land but only after exploiting several individuals including his devoted French-Canadian lover, Yvette, and his idolizing epileptic friend, Virgil, from whom he steals money after Virgil is crippled in an accident while devotedly serving Duddy's business interests. This stock rags-to-riches story is transformed in Richler's hands into a remarkably lively narrative through a brilliant evocation of the Montreal setting, a rich gallery of memorable secondary characters, a number of entertaining comic set pieces, fast-paced action which not only carries the plot forward but provides psychological insights into the characters, and a scintillating portrait of the protagonist.

Not until *The Apprenticeship of Duddy Kravitz*, Richler says, did he develop his own style.[9] An important aspect of this Richlerian style is the pervasive use of humor. Though not absent from the earlier novels, humor, relegated more or less to set scenes, is not integrally associated with the romantic anger of *The Acrobats,* or with the frustration of *Son of a Smaller Hero,* or with the somber dilemma of *A Choice of Enemies.* In *The Apprenticeship of Duddy Kravitz* humor is likewise employed in set scenes such as the screening of Peter Friar's pretentious art film which satirizes artistic affectation and gaucherie, or the commencement exercises at Fletcher's Field where Richler pokes fun at parental rivalries, or the hilarious but inconsequential account of the march of the Fletcher's Field cadets and of Duddy's Warriors deflating a pompous officer of the civil defense corps. However, humor has other, more organic functions in this novel. Richler employs it throughout to aid both his evocation of the earthy society in which Duddy lives and his portrayal of the resilient inhabitants of whom Duddy is one.

Richler's humor is generally not achieved by urbane wit or by the finer points of style. This is not to suggest a lack of skill or subtlety—the use of irony, parody, and the *ingénu* in this and other novels suggests otherwise. But in general the humor here is induced more by incongruity of situation, by absurd invectives and insults, by puns and off-color jokes, and less by verbal twists and polished wit. Such humor is perfectly attuned to and evocative of the world of the novel, for the reader is not in elegant drawing rooms but in tenement surroundings, streets, and bars—an environment where primary and spontaneous feelings are preponderant and are not held under by a veneer of propriety or sophistication.

Richler's humor also underlines what Bernard Schilling considers a characteristic of exiled Jews. Unable to defend themselves physically, they resort to verbal invectives and absurd insults to ease their frustrations. This "comedy of insult," as he describes it, is ludicrously out of proportion to the offense, but "the greater the noise the greater is the relief."[10] Instances of the use of the comedy of insult abound in this and later novels. Perhaps the best illustrations of this in *The Apprenticeship of Duddy Kravitz* are the insults directed against Rubin by the worried patrons at his holiday resort who believe Duddy has drowned himself after his disastrous roulette game. Duddy himself, initially defenseless but persevering in the business world, employs the comedy of insult with an artistic flair. When Cohen, a businessman, refuses to loan him money, this is his response: "Boil in acid, Duddy thought. I hope all your teeth fall out. All except one. And the one that's left should give you a toothache for life" (289). The most important function of humor is to be found in Richler's portrayal of Duddy. Humor enables him to achieve a stronger degree of aesthetic distance and objectivity than is evident in his depiction of the protagonists of the earlier novels. This aesthetic distancing, though commendable, tends to render elusive the exact nature of Richler's attitude to his protagonist, and has occasioned antithetical assessments of his intention in the novel. Some critics believe that he censures Duddy and that his mature objectivity originates from cold satiric detachment. Others feel that he sympathizes with Duddy, and consequently his laughter is not intended to mock but to facilitate control over possible sentimentality.[11] However, as William New and John Ferns have indicated, Richler's attitude is much more complex than this. They correctly perceive an authorial ambivalence at work in his portrait of Duddy. For New, Duddy elicits "a sufferance without approval, an attraction without sympathy, and an attachment without involved concern."[12] Ferns believes that the novel "depends for [its] total effect upon an oscillating pattern of sympathetic and judicial response to its central character. . . . This ultimately involves a double response (not necessarily an ambiguous one) to the novel's conclusion."[13] Richler himself has stated that Duddy is a character whom he both admires and despises.[14] To ignore this ambivalent authorial perception of the protagonist is to respond to the novel as little more than a predictable and straightforward study that simply encourages the reader to take a stand for or against the protagonist. The novel is much more involved than this, however.

Richler creates with strong immediacy the harsh world in which Duddy finds himself. Throughout the novel he sustains a vital tension by portraying with apparently effortless technical control his protagonist at once as a waif of the inescapable conditions of his world and as a youth free to choose his own way of life; and he invites the reader to weigh Duddy's responsibility for his cruel and selfish deeds against his upbringing and environment. Duddy lives in the same place and at the same time as Noah Adler, yet the world of *The Apprenticeship of Duddy Kravitz* is quite different from that of *Son of a Smaller Hero*. Noah's environment is primarily depicted as one that is inhospitable to the aesthete and idealist. Duddy's is a social and business jungle in which only the fittest survive.

Duddy is very much a product of his environment. His father, a part-time pimp, has given him no moral foundation, though he realizes later he should have given Duddy "more of a religious upbringing" (229). When he finds time to instruct him, the paragon he holds up to him is the questionable success of the Boy Wonder. No one else takes time to implant any moral fibre in Duddy. His grandfather, with whom he is closest, suggests a goal in life but not the means by which this should be achieved. Left alone, Duddy responds to his society as a jungle where one must struggle to survive. As a schoolboy he survives by bullying others and by indulging in such dubious business activities as selling pornographic comics and stolen hockey sticks, but when he leaves school for the larger society, he himself confronts exploitation and ridicule. While working at Rubin's resort, he is baited and insulted by the snobbish McGill student, Irwin, a minor character with whose acts of malice for malice's sake Richler, it would appear, deliberately and favorably compares Duddy's conduct. Two businessmen, Uncle Benjy and Cohen, remind Duddy that his world is "a battlefield" (266) in which men "eat each other up" (242). Only sixteen years old at one point in the novel, Duddy is aware that he must awaken prepared for combat: "At ten the next morning Duddy came charging out of a bottomless sleep, unsure of his surroundings but prepared for instant struggle, the alibi for a crime unremembered already half-born, panting, scratching, and ready to bolt if necessary. He shook his head, recognized his room and sighed gratefully" (176). During his intensive struggle to secure his piece of land which the gangster Dingleman wants for himself, Duddy often awakens screaming from a recurring nightmare in which "somebody else's surveyors, carpenters and plumbers roared and hammered and shouted over the land around Lac St. Pierre" (127). In this business jungle, Dingleman treads on the toes of the weaker Duddy who, to survive, must in turn tread on the toes of the yet weaker MacPherson, Yvette, and Virgil.

Even within his family, Duddy finds he must struggle for affection and recognition. With a strict eye on sentimentality, Richler takes pains to convey this unsatisfactory family life. Everyone ignores Duddy and dismisses him as an unpromising cipher, except his aging grandfather who tries feebly to compensate for the indifferent treatment Duddy receives from the others. Max and Uncle Benjy dote on Lennie, the designated doctor of the family. Very early in life Duddy becomes conscious of his father's indifference to him and once anguishingly asks: "Do I always have to be in the wrong? Jeez. Why can't you stick up for me? Just once why can't you . . ." (26). While working at Rubin's resort, Duddy receives no letters or visits from his father and cannot help recalling that when Lennie once worked at a holiday camp his father wrote and visited him regularly. On another occasion Duddy's sensitivity to his family's treatment of him is revealed in his feigned drowning of himself which he hopes will make his father feel "sorry he hadn't treated him as well as Lennie" (90). Toward the end of the novel a relatively older, more cynical Duddy tells his dying Uncle Benjy about his sense of always being unnecessary and unaccommodated within the family: "You know, as a kid I always liked Auntie Ida. But I remember when you used to come to the house you always brought a surprise for Lennie. I could have been born dead as much as you cared" (241). And recalling how Uncle Benjy scorned him when he worked one summer at his factory, he complains bitterly: "I wanted you to like me. You treated me like dirt" (243). Lennie sees his brother simply as a "money-crazy kid" (187) and is ashamed of him. Duddy discovers this when he brags about Lennie's achievements to a McGill student who finds it difficult to accept him as Lennie's brother for "she knew all about Lennie and he had never mentioned that he had a brother" (165). Richler accents the waif in Duddy by having him ask with pathetic recurrence about his deceased mother and particularly about whether she loved him.

Many of the personages in the novel, including Duddy's own family, interpret his relentless and blinkered pursuit of material wealth as the obsession of a "little Jew-boy on the make" (242). The novel, however, indicates that Duddy's obsession with acquiring his piece of land has a deeper origin than just avarice. Duddy is striving for recognition and survival in his belittling community which instills in him a sense of being inconsequential and dispensable. He, who has no chance of succeeding academically or socially, interprets quite literally his grandfather's traditional belief that a man without land is a nobody. He exposes his true motivation in several impassioned outbursts. Once, having been humiliated by Irwin and his privileged friends, Duddy vows to himself: "Maybe I'm dirt today. . . . But you listen here, kiddo. It's not always going to be like this. If you want to bet on something then bet on me. I'm going to be a somebody and that's for sure" (95). To Uncle Benjy, he poignantly expresses his compulsion to prove himself to his unheeding community:

"You lousy intelligent people! You lying sons-of-bitches with your books and your socialism and your sneers. You give me one long pain in the ass. . . . If you're so concerned, how come in real life you never have time for me? . . . You think I should be running after something else besides money? Good. Tell me what. Tell me, you bastard. I want some land, Uncle Benjy. I'm going to own my own place one day. King of the castle, that's me. And there wouldn't be any superior *drecks* there to laugh at me or run me off." (242)

Duddy makes this impassioned outburst to the dying Benjy, who finally perceives Duddy's true motivation when Duddy refuses to accept his generous financial offer which would have made it possible for the desperate youth to make the final payment on Lac St. Pierre. This refusal is crucial when establishing Duddy's character and motivation, for it forces a recognition of the strong possibility that Duddy's desire not just to secure land but to do so *on his own* is an expression of his overwhelming need to prove himself to his belittling community.

Though Richler contemplates Duddy as a child of his environment and circumstances, he is not simply offering him to the reader as a romantic innocent victim of naturalistic forces over which he has little control. The environmental factor is certainly formidable in Duddy's life, but he nevertheless is portrayed as having free will and choice to the extent that he becomes aware of his responsibility for the demise of the MacPherson family and for Virgil's accident, and suffers consequently a nervous breakdown. Duddy's inner life, quite clearly, is not revealed to the reader as incisively or as explicitly as is Noah's in *Son of a Smaller Hero*. This is not because Duddy does not experience conflicts and doubts, but because Richler perceives Duddy as someone constantly externalized, unlike the contemplative Noah, and as having little inner life or little awareness of such a life. Richler himself has commented on Duddy's insufficient perception and sensitivity and his "lack of knowledge" of himself.[15] During his schooldays Duddy creates an imaginary brother, Bradley, a romantically heroic figure, married to a millionairess he rescued from drowning. It becomes apparent that this is done not so much to satisfy the inner craving of an imaginative sensibility but to add to his social stature among his friends—the same way his father draws attention to himself by claiming to be an intimate of the Boy Wonder. His association with Hersh, a minor character patterned after Noah Adler, and with other literary figures satisfies a social rather than an inner yearning. The only work he has read is *God's Little Acre*, his dubious appreciation of which is limited to the sexual scenes.

Duddy's undeveloped inner life is emphasized by Richler's predominant use of the dramatic form of narration—a form appropriate for depicting a character more externalized than internalized. Conversely, *Son of a Smaller Hero* is primarily narrative descriptive, reflecting Noah's introspective nature. Despite Duddy's inability to delve into himself and consciously attempt to examine his feelings like Noah, his conflicts are apparent. His remorse over Mrs. MacPherson's death and Virgil's accident, for both of which he could be held partially responsible, is indicated by dreams and physical actions. Though he denies responsibility for Mrs. MacPherson's death and appears not to have any pricks of conscience, in one of his recurring nightmares he is taken screaming before a judge who turns out to be Mr. MacPherson. His moment of guilt when he forges Virgil's signature is expressed not through conscious expression of feelings but through dramatic action: "Duddy ran, he ran, he ran" (306).

The choices open to Duddy are clearly spelled out at the end of Uncle Benjy's insightful letter to Duddy written on his deathbed:

> There's more to you than mere money-lust, Duddy, but I'm afraid for you. You're two people, that's why. The scheming little bastard I saw so easily and the fine, intelligent boy underneath that your grandfather, bless him, saw. But you are coming of age soon and you'll have to choose . . .
>
> There's a brute inside you, Duddel—a regular behemoth—and this being such a hard world it would be the easiest thing for you to let it overpower you. Don't Duddel. Be a gentleman. A *mensch*. (279)

The brute in Duddy is constantly shown in the novel, much more than the fine qualities his grandfather sees in him. Yet, the reader does observe occasionally the possibilities for good in Duddy. He loves and respects his grandfather, and one of the reasons for acquiring the land around Lac St. Pierre is his desire to provide him with his own piece of land. He selflessly attempts to save Lennie from a dismal future after Lennie performs an illegal abortion, even though his family gives Lennie the praise and recognition denied Duddy. And he equally unselfishly seeks to comfort Aunt Ida and Uncle Benjy when the latter is dying of cancer. Noticeably, Duddy's generous and selfless acts are mainly in his relationship with his family.

He is seldom so considerate with outsiders. This may illustrate Duddy's more immediate yearning for acceptance and recognition by his family, but equally—as is indicated by Noah Adler's similar family relationship—it illustrates the nature of the Jewish ghetto family where family ties remain the touchstone of loyalties and supersede even the most intimate relationship that might develop with individuals outside the family. Here again, Richler presumably is suggesting that Duddy is shaped by the values of his society.

Richler makes Duddy put off reading Uncle Benjy's letter for several days not just to indicate his listlessness after Virgil's accident and Benjy's death, but to await a thematically appropriate occasion to introduce it: Duddy reads the letter at a time when he is not possessed and blinkered by his frantic endeavors to obtain his land and is more capable of objectively considering the two paths open to him that Benjy mentions. He has just recovered from his nervous breakdown—which suggests an apparent rebirth—and is reconciled with Yvette and Virgil with whom he spends a contented week at Yvette's rustic home in Ste. Agathe. He appears to have chosen to be a gentleman and to have rejected the world of Dingleman and Cohen, for when Yvette tells him that the last portion of the lake property is for sale, he is totally unconcerned. However, his reformation is short-lived. On discovering that Dingleman is after Lac St. Pierre, he returns to the jungle and allows the behemoth against which Benjy warned him to overpower him.

In subsequent scenes where Duddy appears knowingly to employ Dingleman's way of life, Richler both tolerates and indicts Duddy. The effect of this tolerance is not to weaken Richler's criticism of Duddy but to increase the tension in the latter part of the novel. Duddy's stealing from Virgil by forging his signature on a check is a reprehensible act, but allowance could be made for him. It is possible to argue that Duddy exhausted every other means of obtaining money in his vicious world before resorting to stealing from Virgil: he borrows or tries to borrow from Cohen, Aunt Ida, his father, and Hugh Calder; he attempts to blackmail Dingleman; and he sells off the furniture Uncle Benjy left him. He also hesitates for a long time before cashing Virgil's check; such qualms never affected him before. He needs the money to realize a dream which Yvette re-introduced into his life when he was with her and Virgil at Ste. Agathe, and he eventually intends to provide financially for Virgil once he acquires his land. Such efforts at justifying Duddy's action, however, do not erase the realization that he has committed a disreputable deed against Virgil and Yvette.

Duddy takes the irrevocable step into Dingleman's world when at the end of the novel he savagely throws the crippled Dingleman off his land. Duddy has taken his family to see his newly acquired property, and Dingleman comes there to congratulate him and to suggest a partnership. Dingleman deserves Duddy's vile abuse, but in treating him in a way so heinous that his own family is appalled, Duddy confirms that he is now a true denizen of the jungle. By chasing Dingleman off his land, Duddy does not reject Dingleman's values, as some critics have suggested,[16] but in fact he begins to embody them more starkly as the new Boy Wonder. Even so, Richler does not encourage any outright condemnation of Duddy. Instead, he chooses to underline the ironies of life inherent in his dubious achievement, for in embracing the false values of the business world Duddy is now the agent as well as the victim of those values. Moreover, Richler invites the reader to consider whether Duddy should choose to survive by adopting the questionable values and succeed by those standards, or refuse to adopt them and go under like many others such as Mac-Pherson, Lennie, and the failed comedian Cuckoo Kaplan.

Though many of the secondary characters have a Dickensian individuality and life of their own, they exist primarily to serve Richler's complex portrayal of his fascinating protagonist. It is possible to put these characters loosely into two antithetical groups which represent the two possibilities continually tugging at Duddy: those that are linked with his potential for good and are more or less favorably portrayed such as Yvette, Duddy's grandfather, Virgil, and Uncle Benjy; and those like the Boy Wonder, Cohen, Friar, and Calder who in various ways and degrees contribute to the surfacing of the brute in him.

Yvette, Duddy's grandfather, and to a lesser extent Virgil represent values that counter those of the inhabitants of the business jungle. They evidently serve as moral agents. As such, however, they are not intended as lifeless symbols. Perhaps this is less true of Yvette, though her failure to come fully alive is the consequence not so much of any intention on Richler's part of making her a morality symbol as of his inability to realize convincingly female characters—which his flat portrait of Miriam in *Son of a Smaller Hero* also reveals. Exactly what in Yvette's psyche motivates her to sacrifice so much for the self-centered Duddy is not satisfactorily explained. In fact, other than a vague hint at sensuality, she appears to have little motivation beyond the requirements of the plot. Devoted, self-sacrificial, honest, altruistic, she walks piously but woodenly through Duddy's life, urging him on with the force of a conscience to an alternative way of life. Virgil, Duddy's other passive victim, is equally unconvincing, and this is primarily because Richler attempts to portray him both as a pathetic figure and as a satiric caricature. As the satire on Virgil's magazine for epileptics and on his poetic efforts shows, Richler—and this is evident often in his novels—is unable to resist a set piece of humor even when inconsistency is the inevitable consequence. Richler's lifeless portraits of Yvette and Virgil in a sense work to his advantage in his effort to balance the reader's response to Duddy. Since these victims of Duddy's obsessive hunt for recognition never really come alive, their suffering at Duddy's hands does not induce close sympathetic identification with them nor does it encourage outright condemnation of Duddy.

Simcha, Duddy's grandfather, is more fully realized and functions more effectively as a moral touchstone than Yvette. He came to Montreal by a quirk of fate rather than by choice. An immigrant from Europe, he was bound for Toronto but his train ticket took him only as far as Montreal, so there he stayed. This quiet acquiescence to circumstances characterizes him and imbues him with a staidness that contrasts with his dissatisfied grandson's frantic scramble. Simcha has a singular honesty and folk wisdom which have earned him the respect of the people in his community. At the end of the novel, he refuses to accept Duddy's gift of a portion of Lac St. Pierre because he abhors the means by which it was acquired. He chooses to stay in his St. Dominique Street backyard, husbanding sour carrots and scrawny corn in the impoverished soil. There is pathos in his stoicism and in the irony of his refusing to accept the land his grandson acquired on his advice, but we cannot help but admire his dignity and uprightness which stand as a constant reprimand of his grandson's villainy.

Uncle Benjy's importance in the novel lies as much in his relationship with the reader as with Duddy. Initially, he appears to be affected and haughty but gradually develops self-knowledge and, toward the end of the novel, becomes on his deathbed the author's mouthpiece, making perceptive comments on Duddy's character but without losing his own separate identity. His insightful comments on himself and on Duddy are as much his own as the author's, for he is an educated, contemplative man in his later life and may well illustrate the Arnoldian observation that truth sits upon the lips of dying men. His unhappy relationship with his wife is introduced to allow another glimpse of Duddy's capacity for generosity and compassion. Duddy makes time in his busy schedule to find Auntie Ida, and as he brings her home to the dying Benjy, he shows much sympathy for this "old woman with a gigolo" (239) whose life disintegrated because of the childless state of her marriage.

Dingleman and Cohen are full-fledged members of the vicious business world against whom Duddy in order to survive must try to be as equally manipulative, callous, and unprincipled. Richler's introduction of these characters serves to show how much worse than the young apprentice's are the vices of these hardened scoundrels. Richler satirically censures both Dingleman and Cohen. In his portrait of the former, the satiric effect is achieved mainly through the incongruity in Max's romanticized, deifying account of Dingleman and the grim ogre he turns out to be when he appears in the novel. Given Dingleman's repulsive character, it is difficult not to applaud Duddy's successful challenging of him at the end of the novel, though the applause quickly fades away when Duddy, taking on Dingleman's values, abuses him as he hobbles away from the lake. The sharpest censure against Cohen occurs in the meeting between Cohen and Duddy after Virgil's accident and Duddy's nervous breakdown. In this extremely skillfully written scene Richler satirically contrasts the avaricious Cohen's self-absorption and expedient attitude toward his fellowman with Duddy's feelings of remorse for the crippled Virgil. Two other figures, Hugh Calder, a Westmount millionaire, and Peter John Friar, a pretentious film director, also contribute to the emergence of the behemoth in Duddy. Duddy finds it necessary to defend himself against Calder's condescension and indulgence toward him, and against Peter John Friar's guile which undoubtedly exceeds Duddy's.

John MacPherson (Duddy's embittered teacher), Lennie, who is victimized by the privileged social circle to which he desperately wants to belong, and Cuckoo Kaplan, the frustrated comedian at Rubin's Laurentian hotel, constitute a third group of characters who, by not tenaciously employing the values of the jungle to defend themselves, are consequently destroyed. Richler acknowledges the pitiful demise of their sustaining ideals and ambitions, particularly MacPherson's. Despite the light digs at their follies, what manifests itself is the tolerance of a writer who has observed that "most of us have jobs we hate and every morning is agony, and that's what life is about . . . in many ways."[17] On the most important level, these three characters represent what would have become of Duddy had he not adopted the ethics of his harsh society. The novel begins with details of MacPherson's youthful ideals, his intensifying frustration, and his eventual despair and madness. Putting the initial emphasis on MacPherson is significant; Richler is persuading the reader to consider whether MacPherson's fate (to which Duddy comes near during his nervous breakdown) is more acceptable than Duddy's survival by adopting the tainted values of his environment.

The novel exhibits a striking correlation between Richler's ambivalent attitude to his protagonist and the structural organization. The overall structure of the novel follows a traditional, linear pattern with Duddy's development traced in four distinct parts. The first part recounts Duddy's boyhood and youth and concludes with the firing of his ambition to own land when he accidentally discovers Lac St. Pierre; the second describes how within six months he acquires half the land; in the third he experiences setbacks and the crisis of Virgil's accident; and in the fourth he realizes his dream. The individual parts, particularly the second, are themselves picaresquely episodic as they follow the boundlessly energetic Duddy from one domestic or business matter to another. There are also several digressive but entertaining set pieces, four of which are set off from the rest of the novel by subheadings: "The March of the Fletcher's Cadets," "Commencement," "The Screening," and "The Crusader," which is further set apart by the use of a different type. In this episodic structuring of the novel one factor touching on Duddy's character is perceivable: Richler loosely alternates scenes of Duddy's selflessness in his relationship with his family and of his victimization by others such as Irwin and Dingleman with scenes where his selfishness and callousness are prominent. As the novel progresses, this alternating pattern becomes more evident and encourages a seesawing, binary response to the young rogue.

The outstanding aspect of *The Apprenticeship of Duddy Kravitz* is Richler's scintillating portrait of Duddy. It is a remarkable achievement on Richler's part that he succeeds in not making Duddy repellent when he shows his vices and in not rendering him a sentimental figure when he portrays him as one who cannot avoid being molded by his environment. Richler, aware of both the worst and the possibilities for good in his protagonist, is neither his castigator nor his advocate. He does not intend that the reader should simply identify with Duddy or unquestioningly reject him. Such responses would be a gross simplification of Richler's achievement. Were Duddy a real-life acquaintance of the reader it is true that he would be on his guard against Duddy; however, with Duddy safely contained between the covers of the novel, Richler invites the reader to look objectively at him, though, like the author, he may not be able to affirm whether he admires or despises him.

Chapter Three
The Political Novels:
The Acrobats and
A Choice of Enemies

Like *Son of a Smaller Hero*, *The Acrobats* and *A Choice of Enemies* are concerned with a search for principles and absolutes in a world where there is no "agreed-upon system of values."[1] While Noah Adler undertakes his quest within the changing Jewish ghetto of Montreal, André Bennett of *The Acrobats* and Norman Price of *A Choice of Enemies* conduct theirs in postwar Europe where Richler perceives causes and ideologies to be the principal factors informing human relationships. Though several of the secondary characters in these two novels function essentially as mouthpieces for political creeds, the author does not concentrate on abstract political machinations or on the corridors of power, choosing instead to examine how ideological and political issues affect the lives of individuals. Exposed to various causes and beliefs, Richler's two ambivalent protagonists, whose sensibilities vary only slightly from that of the sensitive and intense Noah, become very indecisive and are no longer sure what is evil or good, what should be censured or sanctioned, and whether in fact they are escapees or searchers. Their state of mind is clearly pointed up by the richly suggestive titles of the novels.

The Acrobats

The Acrobats was accepted for publication in 1953, but before it was actually published, Richler revised portions of it fairly extensively on the suggestion of his editors and agent. At least three revisions were undertaken, and after the third, Richler wrote to his publisher saying: "I am no longer truly involved with *The Acrobats* and am wary of doing too much tampering. If I were to rewrite the book completely I might be able to make it a better, more artistic work. But, on the other hand, I might ruin whatever spontaneity it has. At this point, I think it would be far better to apply what I have learnt off this book to the one I am now working on."[2] The spontaneous overflow of powerful—sometimes adolescent—feelings is perhaps the main merit of this impressive but flawed first novel. However, as Richler realized even as he sent off his revised manuscript to the publisher, the novel could have profited from further revision which might have allowed Richler to eliminate (as he did in subsequent novels) the two main shortcomings: the subservience of character development to thematic aims and the unabsorbed echoes of writers such as Dos Passos, Hemingway, and Malraux. *The Acrobats* is not wholly satisfying on its own, but, as the incubator of many thematic and stylistic aspects of the later novels, it is a fascinating apprenticeship work.

Though the novel has a fair number of characters and incidents, narrative progression and action are minimal and are generally conscripted to explore the protagonist's involved inner experiences. The main narrative relates the experiences in Franco's postwar Spain of a young but already world-weary Canadian painter, André Bennett, who, when the novel opens, is living in a rat-infested hotel in Valencia. He has apparently run away from a privileged but tedious life with his wealthy father and his socialite mother. The immediate reason for his escape to Spain, however, is the traumatic resolution of his bitter love affair with a Jewish girl, Ida Blumberg, who, pregnant by him, died at the hands of an abortionist. In Spain André befriends several working-class Spaniards and finds some comfort with Toni, a young prostitute. His intention of marrying this child-woman, orphaned by the war, is frustrated by a jealous rival, Roger Kraus, a Nazi on the run, who shadows him night and day and eventually kills him. After André's death, Toni manages to escape to Paris with Chaim, a kind-hearted, elderly Jew, who himself flees Spain because Kraus informs the authorities of his forged passport. Toni marries an American who learns from Chaim that her newborn baby, though named after André, was in fact fathered by Kraus.

This main narrative takes up just over half the novel. The other half introduces several minor characters and insubstantial minor plots: Guillermo, a communist guerilla whom André befriends, is hunted and caught by Franco's soldiers—all happening offstage; Pepe and Maria, an impoverished couple, are expecting a baby who is born at the end of the novel; Theresa, Kraus's sister, once involved with Nazi concentration camps, commits suicide, apparently because of her empty life and belated remorse over her betrayal of a Jewish lover; Barney Larkin, an insensitive Jewish-American businessman visits Valencia with his sensual gentile wife, Jessie, who tries to seduce André; Jessie's brother, Derek, a communist soldier during the Civil War, is now disillusioned with what has happened to Spain and seeks solace with homosexual partners like Juanito, a pimp who claims to be a university student and daydreams of political power. These incidents and characters only tenuously complicate and advance the action of the novel. They are more significant to Richler's evocation of the Spanish ethos and to his study of his tormented protagonist.

Richler's structural organization of the main narrative and the several minor plots show him adhering from this first novel to his artistic credo that the good writer must be an entertainer as well as a moralist. He arranges his material in such a way that the reader's curiosity is ignited and suspense sustained. Early in the book, for instance, he arouses interest in the reason for André's being shadowed, in the extent of André's involvement in the death of Ida, and in the identity of the father of Toni's child. The novel, characteristically, is episodic, but Richler tries to lace these episodes together by compressing the action (except for the Afterwards) into three days and by narrating André's earlier experiences concurrently through flashbacks and retrospections—a technique more ambitiously employed in *St. Urbain's Horseman* and *Joshua Then and Now*. The structure of *The Acrobats* anticipates also the dialectic progression of some of the later novels. Richler alternates and juxtaposes various episodes to serve his study of antithetical ideologies and values rather than to achieve linear narrative progression. For instance, juxtaposed episodes contrast the fascist Kraus with the humane André, the materialist Barney's visit to a gross brothel with André's warm lovemaking to Toni, and the active communist guerrilla, Guillermo, with Derek, the impotent and disillusioned communist veteran.

One of the strengths of *The Acrobats* is Richler's powerful evocation of the Spanish setting through his vivid recall of sensuous impressions. He captures well the mood and spirit of Valencia of the 1950s. In an early scene, the whirling atmosphere of the Spanish fiesta and the oppressive poverty, which sharply set off each other, are effectively evoked despite Richler's dependence on Hemingway's clean, sharp prose, on variations of Dos Passos's newsreel, camera eye, and biographies, and on Joyce's stream of consciousness. The young novelist unleashes surging imagery and diction which become poetic prose, occasionally mannered and cloying, but more often quite effective. Here, echoing Hemingway, he captures the draining exuberance of the frenzied fiesta dancers:

> They danced until their bodies ached from excess of pleasure (and they thought the earth had fallen out of the sky), they danced until their eyes were swollen with need of sleep (and they saw the buildings were of gold and the streets of soft silk and the lamp posts lit by glowing diamonds), they danced until they were too drunk to stand (and they believed the sun was hot and the earth was friendly and the grass was green in spring), they danced until Sunday's dawn filled the sky gloomily and without promise (and they believed in the day and God and they were no longer afraid).[3]

Through more measured and exact prose, Richler conveys André's experience of Valencia's brutal poverty:

> In his anxiety to keep on moving, not to see, he nearly stumbled over a crippled beggar. Both the man's legs had been severed at the knees: a filthy cotton material was wound around the stumps. He was sprawled out in the street singing an imbecile tune, his skinny arms outstretched as if awaiting crucifixion. Spread out before him in the grime was a weird conglomeration of goods—tobacco, matches, flints, prophylactics, crucifixes, and two tattered novels by Zane Grey. A ragged dog was sniffing at the edge of his tiny universe of wares. Quite suddenly the beggar gave him a swift wallop in the ribs with a clenched fist. Then he began to cackle idiotically, yellow spittle trickling down the sides of his mouth. Several of the passing soldiers and whores joined in the merriment. André followed the track of the dog as he raced down the street amid a shower of kicks. (29–30)

Richler's talent for depicting setting graphically and evocatively is evident here. His images are sharp and insistent (particularly the ironical picture of the mindless cruelty of the beggar who himself elicits pity) and persuade us to feel, not just observe, the harsh existence of Valencia's poor.

Richler presents this postwar environment primarily through André's consciousness, and, as in *Son of a Smaller Hero*, he tends to blur slightly his portrait of his protagonist by not standing sufficiently apart from him, particularly from his feverish intensity and romantic notions. This becomes readily evident if the novel is juxtaposed with the parts of *Joshua Then and Now* that relate the experiences of young Joshua, who, like André, makes a trip to Spain in the

1950s, befriends the Spaniards, falls in love, and heroically attempts to challenge an opponent who appears to be a former Nazi. In the later novel Richler stands comfortably apart from both the young and the mature Joshua who, reviewing his life at the age of forty-seven, is able to perceive his youthful idealistic judgments and righteous indignation for what they were.

Like Hemingway's characters in *The Sun Also Rises,* Richler's personages, three decades later, live their inner lives publicly in sidewalk cafés, bars, streets, and bedrooms that are as much meeting places as retreats. This, of course, was the face of the society visible to the young novelist during his brief stay in Spain. Unlike Hemingway, however, Richler does not penetrate to the essence of his characters' publicly lived inner experiences. Unfamiliar with the psyche of most of his various personages, he inevitably renders them one-dimensionally and aggravates this by overburdening many of them, such as Guillermo, Derek, and Kraus, with political and ideological significance. Causes and issues preoccupy his characters, minor as well as major, whether they are making love or dancing, sipping wine in nightclubs or viewing the fiesta displays, anticipating the birth of a child or watching a man die.

André's characterization suffers from the novel's preoccupation with the political and the ideological. Though the central character, he is narrowly depicted as someone obsessed by causes and beliefs. This obsession influences virtually all his relationships and dominates his conversations and discussions. André's portrayal becomes briefly animated when Richler refers to his empty life in Canada: his cold filial relationship with a bohemian mother whom he dubs *"la belle Lucretia"* (55) and a distant father who doubts André is his son; his miserable life at university where he found it necessary to buy friendship; and his fleeting moment of happiness with Ida, whom he loved intensely. These experiences in Canada are given in occasional flashbacks and recollections and are certainly not as prominent an aspect of André's life in Spain as is his absorption with ideologies. André is bedeviled by migraines, insomnia, nightmares, and intimations of madness, the source of which appears to be not so much his traumatic experiences in Canada as his weariness and perplexity with the contemporary political situation.

Richler conveys the nature of André's perplexity quite directly in frequent and extended discursive comments—a method that the author later viewed unfavorably: "I think that for an idea to be artistically valid, it should never be stated but should always be implied through a character."[4] While André, the depressed lover and son, comes to Spain to escape his miserable life in Canada, André, the politically conscious youth, comes to Valencia, once the capital of the Loyalist Government now impoverished and squalid, because of his admiration for the heroic International Brigades who committed themselves to the defense of Spain and who, because of their dedication to their cause, come to epitomize for André honor and truth, virtues he considers to be lacking in his own age. But he is disillusioned by the subsequent actions of these once-idealistic men who "had proven either duds or counterfeits—standing up in the thirties to cheer the revolution hoarsely, and in the fifties sitting down again to write a shy, tinny, blushing yes to capitalistic democracy" (29). Faced with this disappointment, André's vision darkens: ". . . he had grown up to find all Gods dead, all wars fought, all faiths in men shaken. There was going to be another war all right . . ." (29). Despite this pessimism, however, he simultaneously retains an idealistic belief in the possibility of finding the absolute truth: "There was *the* truth, a shining beauty of a truth, and if he was strong enough he would find it. But until then, until that never day, his centre would be confusion" (56).

Richler's examination of André's relationship with many of the individuals he meets in Valencia such as the lapsed communist Derek, the current communist Guillermo, the capitalist Barney, and the facist Kraus serves to emphasize his quandary. André in his indecisive state of mind responds ambivalently to these characters as he gets to know them better. In his relationship with Derek he discovers that this American poet, who dedicated himself to the Spanish cause both in battle and in his poems, cynically rejects communism and in fact fears that "the tyranny of the proletariat will exceed the boorishness of the petty-bourgeois" (121), a pronouncement that André does not dismiss out of hand since he recalls the brutal actions of some of Guillermo's indigent followers, the very figures who, once glorified and idealized by the writers of the 1930s, now ridicule their would-be liberators. While chatting with André, Guillermo casts doubts on Derek's idealistic motives for participating in the civil war, asserting that he, like others of his social sphere, "got bored with the cocktail parties in New York so they came over for the party in Spain" (65). André shares Guillermo's anger at the poverty and misery spawned by Franco's regime; but Toni, whose parents and brother lost their lives in the civil war, tries to convince him that Guillermo's commitment to revolutionary violence makes him capable only of destruction.

Barney, a stereotype of the vulgar American tourist of the 1950s, embodies the antithetical political concept of capitalism. Like the other adherents to ideas and causes, he constantly and explicitly declares his beliefs to the reader: "I don't see why if I worked so hard all my life so that I could have it easy when I was old I should give my money to guys who were just too lazy to sweat like me. Do you think communism is fair? It's sort of robbery in a way" (149). Richler quickens Barney's characterization—at least more than that of the other minor characters—by giving him a personal life outside the political sphere. His crass materialism is announced in most scenes, but there are accounts of his wretched mixed marriage, his conflict with his traditional Jewish way of life, his sexual neuroses, and his need for self-esteem. In some respects, he is an early outline for the more complex Duddy Kravitz. His outburst, for instance, against his intellectual brother-in-law is similar in substance, diction, and tone to Duddy's against Uncle Benjy: "Why do you always treat me as if I was a jerk? . . . I know what you people think. I'm vulgar, I haven't had an education. I never read any books. Everything I've done I had to do for myself . . ." (147). Like Duddy also, Barney elicits a mixed response from Richler who, though he presents him unattractively in most scenes, still shows some tolerance. Commenting outside the novel on Barney, Richler confirms this counterpointing sympathy for him when he describes him as someone "perpetually misunderstood and misunderstanding."[5]

Kraus is more involved in the main narrative than any of the other secondary characters for he is André's rival for Toni's love. Despite this narrative involvement, however, Richler's depiction of him and of the characters of the triangular love affair continues to subsume their personal feelings beneath their ideological roles. The rivalry between André and Kraus is provoked not so much by the jealousy of lovers but by political differences—André representing a vague idealistic humanism and Kraus a mindless fascism. On another level, Richler uses them as alter egos to explore the duality of human nature and the relationship between the man of action and the contemplative artist—a theme which he explores through a similar use of alter egos in *St. Urbain's Horseman*. The oneness of these opponents is suggested several times. André, for instance, has a violent, impulsive streak

seen in his harsh treatment of Ida's father, in his physical attack on
Kraus at the Mocambo Club, and in *his* threats to kill Kraus. Kraus
is afraid of André because he sees himself in him. Toni appears to
respond to these figures as dual aspects of one person. And André
himself clearly recognizes Kraus to be a part of his own psyche when
he confronts him on the bridge just before his death.

But there are major differences between these two. The contemplative André, hopeless and directionless, knows he must try to act, for
"not to act would mean non-living" (56); yet he admits, "I don't
know what to do" (67). Kraus is depicted as the very opposite. A
mechanical being, trained by the Nazis to carry out orders, he acts
without thinking. When he kills André, it is not entirely through
his own motivation but on the order of his sister, a former Nazi official, who describes him as a "little, wooden soldier" (178). Despite
Kraus's vicious character, Richler tries to present him understand-
ingly. Without a country and on the run, he is ironically Jewish.
Once a proud soldier, he is reduced to running messages and smuggling for a Jew by whom he feels threatened. His only solace is his
belief in fascism, but even this is denied him when he learns that his
sister, on whom he is emotionally dependent, never truly believed in
Nazism. Kraus springs from the author's own meeting with a Nazi
in Spain. Richler's account of this incident reveals a relationship between himself and the German which, though not firmly duplicated
in the novel, is hinted at in his attempt at a balanced portrait of
Kraus:

> I met the man, a tall German, in a bodega. He asked me when I had last
> seen Paris and I told him. "And you?" I asked.
> "I left with the S.S. in 1944."
> I laughed.
> "I'm under sentence of death in France for war crimes," he said.
> I drank again and laughed some more. Foolishly.
> "A war's a war," he said.
> "Sure," I said.
> Afterwards we went to his hotel to get a bottle. There was a signed pic-
> ture by his bedside. "Say," I said, picking it up, "that looks like
> Mussolini."
> "Mussolini was a man just like any other man," he said. "He had his
> faults."
> Finally, it reached me, that the man wasn't joking. He had been in the
> S.S. A colonel. He had also fought with France in Spain. I based the char-
> acter of Colonel Roger Kraus, in *The Acrobats*, on this man.[6]

André's death at the hands of Kraus is one of the scenes Richler's editor suggested omitting. But Richler, convinced that the protagonist's death grows out of the plot and that it functions as "a symbol in itself,"[7] insisted on retaining it. The confrontation between the two rivals for Toni's love does grow out of the plot, but it does not necessarily have to end in André's death. Just before his death, André the lover is willing to flee with Toni to Paris, thus avoiding any confrontation with Kraus. But his function as a symbolic or perhaps an allegorical figure supersedes that as a person and requires that he should meet his death on the bridge just when the largest falla bursts into flames. What exactly does his death allegorize? This is a difficult question, for André's death is apparently one of three resolutions with which the young novelist awkwardly contrives to conclude the novel, and which illustrates what Nathan Cohen describes as Richler's "unsettling ambivalence of thought."[8] The other two resolutions are the birth of Pepe's and Maria's baby in the final section of the novel proper (that is, before the Afterwards) and the appended ending in the Afterwards which tells of the birth of Toni's baby and of her coming marriage to an American, a blatant *deus ex machina*.

André's death quite likely indicates how difficult it is for the idealist and humanist to challenge a world made and dominated by Krauses. The occurrence of his death simultaneously with the burning of the giant falla, an inanimate scapegoat of the fiesta ceremony, suggests also that he is a sacrifice for humanity—an observation supported by Chaim's remark that André's killer was "the instrument of us all" (188). In the Afterwards ending Toni's baby is obviously a symbol of hope. Fathered by Kraus and named after André, the child would appear to represent a future in which brutality is controlled by humaneness and obsessive contemplation is balanced by will and action.

The third resolution grows more organically out of the narrative and thematic requirements of the novel. Pepe and Maria, the parents of the baby born a few hours after André's death in the last section of the novel proper, abhor politics and are warm, generous, unprejudiced, and full of hope in spite of the poverty and violence that enfold them. They become André's devoted friends and are solicitous about his welfare not because of any political kinship but because he is a lonely and perturbed fellow being. They embody Chaim's rejection of ideologies: "There is no idea or cause that will save us all. Salvation is personal" (107). These sentiments are endorsed by Richler outside the novel: "You know we can no longer hope or only a fool can hope for revolution as a solution to anything. Increasingly we know each system contains its own injustices. . . ."⁹ Chaim then, at least here, is Richler's mouthpiece and provides one of the thematic resolutions of the novel. His wisdom is given clearer symbolic expression in the birth of Pepe's and Maria's baby than in André's death, for André dies raging against an ideological enemy with little self-awareness and no clear affirmation of any moral or political position.

Richler's account of André's relationship with the various residents of Valencia reveals his early talent for constructing dramatic scenes and for conveying characterization by distinctness of speech, of which the reader becomes increasingly aware in the later novels. On occasion, however, as George Bowering observes, Richler's dialogue becomes too mannered and too self-conscious.¹⁰ Significantly, most of these instances of contrived conversation are generally the consequence of Richler's imposing political comments on his characters. In this scene, for instance, where Pepe is comforting his ailing, pregnant wife, the thematic requirement of the novel forces itself into their conversation:

"Why did he die, Maria? What did it mean?"
"I don't know."
"But you're religious. You believe these things happen for a reason."
A man was banging on a drum. The window pane rattled. My son is in her belly, Pepe thought, and it is warm and snug for him.
"It is not enough to say that he died for a cause. Nobody dies for a cause. They die for their women and their family. And he wanted to live for them," Pepe said.
She said nothing.
"Remember? He used to look so funny when he laughed."
"Maybe he died for you?"
He found her solemn face in the dark. Her deep black eyes were without expression and her lovely lips were quiet.
"For me?"
"So that you might understand something."
"What?"
"I don't know." (26–27)

The scene is overwritten particularly toward the end where Richler attempts to use the characters' solemnity to suggest profundity of feelings and thoughts. The dramatic portrayals of the personal apolitical experiences of the characters, such as Barney's unhappy mixed marriage and Chaim's resignation to living a life of exile, are much more convincing.

Set pieces of satire, so characteristic of Richler's later works, are encountered in this first novel. There are in fact just two such passages in *The Acrobats*. One is a very brief censure of Canadian "Kultchir" (72), which perhaps is less a cogent satirical disgression on Canada than an illustration of André's emotional turmoil and of his ambivalence, for, as Toni perceives, his "anger against his family and his country comes of love" (57). The other is set off by italic type and is quite clearly digressive and satirical. It censures the responses to the frenzied fiesta dance of four dignitaries (an unidentified ambassador, an American representative, the Archbishop of Valencia, and one of Franco's generals) who, closing their eyes to the ubiquitous poverty aound them, sit aloof from the dancers waiting to be entertained. Richler's main satiric technique is to juxtapose the antithetical responses of the dignitaries with those of the common people. He sets their stereotyped comments against the passionate revolutionary songs of the fiesta crowd, their orchestrated dancing against the spontaneity of the street dancers, and their chitchat against a child begging inaudibly in the crowd. The satiric effect is heightened by Richler's use of the anaphoric phrase *"The Ambassador laughed heartily"* (37) and of the parody of the Social Register in his brief biography of the American representative—a technique which he employs more extensively in *St. Urbain's Horseman* to satirize the English lawyer, Ormsby-Fletcher.

The importance of this first novel, which Richler protectively describes as his "most vulnerable"[11] book, lies more in what it promises for the author's career than in what it actually achieves. There is undeniably some appeal in its honest and intense youthful perceptions, its evocation of mood, its portrayal of a few distinct personages, and its frequent energetic use of language, but the many flaws prevent it from being a wholly satisfying accomplishment on its own. It remains essentially a useful means by which to measure the extent of Richler's progress as an artist.

A Choice of Enemies

A Choice of Enemies is largely *The Acrobats* rewritten three years later. The narrative, the pattern of relationship among characters, the dominant and the subsidiary themes, the ambiance of politics, and

the protagonists' ambivalence which induces emotional and spiritual
malaise are similar in both novels. Richler avoids certain shortcomings of the earlier work: the impassioned tone is more modulated,
characterization is more subtle, derivative passages are eliminated,
and the theme is not shouted at the reader. But Richler has not suc-
ceeded in ironing out all the wrinkles of *The Acrobats,* and, like that
novel, *A Choice of Enemies* belongs to Richler's novitiate, or perhaps to
the transitory span between apprenticeship and maturity. The narrative is often contrived and occasionally melodramatic; certain characters are wooden and overtly subservient to the political theme; and
the unraveling of the novel is still a bit awkward. As with *The Acrobats,* Richler himself was very much aware of the novel's faults before
its publication and was dissatisfied enough with his final draft to
consider recalling the novel when it was virtually already between
covers. [12]

A *Choice of Enemies,* like *The Acrobats,* examines the experiences of
various political émigrés in postwar Europe, but while the earlier
novel is set in Valencia, *A Choice of Enemies* is set in London. There
are several parallels between the main characters and their relationships in the two novels. The triangular love affair of André, Toni,
and Kraus, which constitutes the main plot of the earlier novel, has its
counterpart in that of Norman Price, Sally MacPherson, and Ernst
Haupt. Norman, the protagonist, is a Canadian professor who fled
McCarthy's inquisition while teaching at an American university and,
when the novel opens, has been residing in London where he makes
a living writing thrillers and film scripts. Sally is a guileless young
woman who has come to London from Canada to broaden her experience. And Ernst is a desperate, unprincipled refugee from East Germany who, on his way to London, unintentionally kills Norman's
brother, Nicky, stationed at an American base in Germany. The love
affair, like its counterpart in *The Acrobats,* ends unhappily for all
concerned. Norman loses Sally to Ernst who flees to Montreal when
Norman discovers him to be Nicky's murderer, and soon after he conveniently marries a rich widow. Abandoned, Sally becomes the mistress of one of the émigrés and eventually commits suicide.

Many of the secondary characters of *The Acrobats* reappear in different guises in this novel. Derek and the other communist intellectuals,
a prime source of André's disillusionment, have their counterparts in
Winkleman's coterie of Hollywood expatriates, who are victims of
McCarthy's witch hunt, and among whom are some veterans of the

Spanish Civil War. These men, who chose to exile themselves voluntarily rather than betray friends to McCarthy's Un-American Activities Committee, are ironically shown persecuting Ernst, a fellow exile and political refugee—but from East German communism; because Norman befriends Ernst, the Winkleman crowd ostracizes him. Barney's marital and social problems in *The Acrobats* are now those of Norman's friend, Charlie Lawson, an untalented Canadian scriptwriter who struggles for social acceptance and for the love of his wife. Charlie's experience is given more scope than Barney's; Richler tells of his total dependence for scriptwriting opportunities on Norman whom he comes to resent, of his misinforming on Norman to the Winkleman crowd, and of his eventual return to Canada where he becomes an important television personality. The Chaim figure of *The Acrobats* is transformed from a kind, wise old man into the psychotic, vengeful, physically repulsive Karp, a former concentration camp quisling who betrays Norman by hinting to Charlie and Winkleman that Norman is an informer. Toni's marriage at the end of *The Acrobats* parallels the marriage of Norman who, unable to cope with his rejection by Sally, Winkleman's crowd, and Charlie, develops temporary amnesia and is nursed back to health by an English girl, Vivian Bell, whom he marries in the final chapter of the novel.

These various relationships and narrative strands are more elaborately developed and more effectively intertwined than they are in *The Acrobats*, and they further affirm Richler's increasing interest in holding the reader's attention with involved plotting. At crucial points in the narrative, however, the plot appears to be too contrived and too harnessed to Richler's study of the effects on the individual of involvement with political causes. The central complication is transparently engineered: Ernst, the murderer of Norman's brother in Germany, by chance meets Sally in London, through whom he gets to know Norman. Norman is set on introducing Ernst, inexperienced in film making, to Winkleman's Hollywood coterie supposedly, on the narrative level, to secure for Ernst employment and social acceptance, but quite evidently it is the technique by which Richler precipitates the moral crisis. The resolution of the main narrative is equally factitious. Norman manages to meet his future bride, Vivian, a *deus ex machina* figure like Toni's fiancé at the end of *The Acrobats*, because he is unable to establish who he is during his attack of amnesia; and this is because the preceding night, though distraught, he conveniently emptied his pockets of all possible identification in getting his clothes ready for the laundry. Sally dies because her lover, Landis, is prevented fortuitously from making his clockwork visit to her apartment by Norman's unexpected appearance at Landis's home. Consequently, he does not reach Sally in time, as she expected, to prevent her suicide, which she really intended as a ploy to dissuade Landis from forcing her to abort her pregnancy. In the meantime, Ernst in Montreal just happens to be at the right place to prevent, at the risk of his own life, a businessman from being crushed to death by a falling building—a heroic deed which wins him social acceptance and a rich North American widow. He is blackmailed into marrying this unscrupulous woman who somehow happens to know of Ernst's illegal entry into Canada, an ironically appropriate but contrived conclusion to Ernst's story. Such instances of patent plot manipulation tend to bear out Richler's observation just before the publication of *A Choice of Enemies* that he worries more about people than about plot when he writes his novels. [13]

The portrayal of the people of *A Choice of Enemies* is much better done than in the earlier work. In the first instance, Richler achieves an aesthetic distancing from his protagonist that was missing in *The Acrobats* and *Son of a Smaller Hero*. He stands apart from Norman and appraises him fairly objectively. Though the contrived narrative invites skepticism at certain points about the psychological credibility of their motivation, most of the characters are not merely mouthpieces of political creeds like their counterparts in *The Acrobats*. They tend to be more flesh and blood. However, they still lack the vibrant aliveness of characters in such novels as *The Apprenticeship of Duddy Kravitz* or *St. Urbain's Horseman*. Richler's constant shifting of focus from the individual human relationships to the political issues is largely responsible for this. In the account of Norman's relationship with his exiled North American compatriots, for instance, Richler examines Norman's tormenting ambivalence; like Noah, he is caught between accepting and rejecting his environment. But Richler is also set on proving, as he himself has stated, that the émigrés' "whole left-wing quarrel" with McCarthy was "less of an argument of principle and more of an argument of power," and that they cared not for freedom of speech and belief but for "*their* freedom of speech and *their* democratic rights." [14]

Richler portrays Norman as someone who, like André, is preoccupied with the political and ideological problems of his time. He yearns for what he considers the political absolutes of the 1930s and for his father's firm convictions that led him to give up his lucrative Montreal medical practice to fight and die in Spain. However, Norman, who is thirty-eight years old when the novel opens, is not as bewildered politically as young André. He shares his father's belief in Marxism for which he unhesitatingly sacrifices his fairly secure job as a professor. But he is beginning to question his and his colleagues' political sincerity: "You signed petitions, you defended Soviet art to liberals, and you didn't name old comrades. But your loyalties, like those of a shared childhood, were sentimental; they lacked true conviction."[15] Norman has given up his party membership, but remains a Marxist through force of habit and need for a sense of social belonging rather than because of unswerving conviction. He is an even-tempered, contemplative man, who, to prevent lapses into amnesia, with which he has been afflicted since his plane crashed when he was an RCAF pilot during World War II, must keep his life free from disturbances. And so he consciously avoids confrontation and difficult decisions. Though he is aware of the absurdities and vices of those around him, he tries his utmost to be conciliatory and tolerant and reprimands himself, like Jake Hersh of *St. Urbain's Horseman,* whenever he fails to do so. The advent of Ernst into his life, however, forces him for a while into a painful revaluation of his beliefs and into undertaking another Richlerian quest for some acceptable form of truth.

Norman's awakening to the true nature of his compatriots occurs in the climactic scene of the novel where Ernst is treated viciously by the North American exiles at Winkleman's party. Richler uses this scene in particular to underline the ironical parallel between McCarthy's treatment of those suspected of being communist sympathizers and their treatment of Ernst. At one point during the party, Colin Horton, a highly skilled journalist, the latest McCarthy victim, mercilessly interrogates Ernst, encouraged by other members of Winkleman's clique. This provokes Norman who has brought Ernst to the party hoping his friends would accept a fellow refugee:

"Look," Norman said, "most of us were on the hot seat at home. Don't you recognise Horton's technique of questioning?"

"Really," Horton said, "this is too much. Are you accusing me of being a McCarthyite?"

"That's just what I mean. Remarks like that," Norman said. "Twisting my words to his own purpose." (85)

Richler, perhaps too insistently, keeps returning to the ironical parallel with McCarthyism in this and subsequent scenes. When Horton returns from his tour of the communist countries, for instance, his pejorative comment on McCarthy's methods accurately describes the émigrés' suspicion of Norman's motive in associating with Ernst: "I explained that most of the informers were psychopaths and that one never got a chance to face one's accusers . . ." (134). Charlie Lawson's betrayal is another fairly obvious parallel. Hoping to ingratiate himself with the Winkleman crowd, he insinuates that Norman has become an informer. He does attempt to protest Norman's innocence on realizing the enormity of his betrayal, but his protest dissipates once he gains social parity with the group and is assured employment by them.

Norman's rejection of his compatriots at Winkleman's party, pointed up by his resorting to physical violence to defend Ernst (which is his only impetuous and spontaneous act in the novel), jerks him briefly out of his ambivalent frame of mind. But almost immediately he begins "to feel the sands shift under him" (95). Not only is he ostracized and denied work by his former friends, but more important, he finds himself in a state of ennui, with no firm beliefs and no values. His mental and emotional quandary brings on an attack of amnesia. On regaining his memory—which Richler offers as an indication of his rebirth—he comes to believe, like Chaim of *The Acrobats,* that the solution to human problems is not to be found in politics. What is important in life is not involvement in ideologies and alliances but adherence to "small virtues" (215), to the traditional spiritual values of honesty, goodness, and honor in one's everyday relationship with one's fellowman:

If there was a time to man the barricades, Norman thought, then there is also a time to weed one's private garden. . . . This was a time to drop a nickel in the blind man's box and to recommend worthwhile movies to strangers. . . . The enemy was no longer the boor in power on the right or the bore out of power on the left. (215)

One of the episodes in the novel that has puzzled critics is Norman's concern during his attack of amnesia for a child's balloon lodged in the ceiling of Waterloo Air Terminal. Richler's extended treatment of this incident suggests that it is intended as more than simply an illustration of Norman's mental illness. Graeme Gibson sees Norman's obsession with the balloon as his search for a lost state of innocence. [16] It could also be interpreted as Norman's growing awareness of the importance of what Richler calls "small decencies"[17] in human relationships which appear to be of little significance next to the great causes and movements. Norman's conversation about the balloon with a busy man who, ironically, is reading Norman Vincent Peale's column in *Look,* particularly suggests this interpretation:

> "Did you notice the balloon before I sat down to tell you about it?"
> "Nope."
> "What do you think they ought to do about it?"
> "I don't want to sound unneighbourly, but frankly speaking, son, I've got bigger worries."
> "That's not the point." (160)

Adhering to his new credo, Norman resolves "at last to lead a private life" (215). His first act in accordance with his new resolution is to let Ernst, his brother's murderer, "go in peace. Let him be" (215). And, like Noah Adler, though he leaves the environment to which he once belonged, he does so with no bitterness. He is aware of his friends' shortcomings but also of their sacrifice for their convictions and of their generosity to him when, as a refugee himself, he needed a sense of belonging. Toward the end of the novel Norman meets Horton, who has now become aware of Stalin's brutality, and the once-pompous advocate of communism is now disillusioned with Marxism. Norman sympathizes with him and sees him as another casualty of blind faith in ideologies. In the final chapter Norman resolves to return to teaching in a provincial university, work on his book on Dryden, become a father, invite friends to dinner, and try to cope with his wife's social aspirations.

The account of the new society to which Norman attaches himself through his marriage to Vivian is far too sketchy to allow the reader to establish satisfactorily whether Norman adheres to his stated credo in his new life or whether this credo is simply a resolution of the political theme with little relevance to the protagonist's actual life in the novel. The most extended account of Vivian's society is in the final chapter which tells of the wedding reception. Even here, Norman's credo is not dramatically displayed, for the scene is peopled by characters who are drawn essentially as caricatures and types: "All the gay, sophisticated men gathered in his flat could be divided into two groups. Those who wore extravagant waistcoats and those who went in for extravagant moustaches" (212). Vivian herself verges on caricature and is too obviously a device. Such figures deny the possibility of any convincing demonstration of Norman's resolution to adhere to small virtues.

The absence of any such dramatic illustration of Norman's credo in these final scenes has encouraged critical dispute about the ending of the novel. Bruce Stovel believes that Norman "fights his way back to an honest self-scrutiny, to a separate peace, to a determination to struggle for success in his marriage and his work."[18] Kerry Mc-Sweeney and Nathan Cohen do not share this positive view of Norman. McSweeney finds that Norman is "a worn out, morally numbed man passively sinking into a marital limbo with a shallow, opportunistic and ugly wife."[19] And Cohen, pointing to the pretensions, vanities, and rivalries of Vivian's society, states that "Norman Price simply exchanges one bickering, demeaning world for another."[20] It is possible to see the ending of the novel both ways, primarily because of the two discrete levels on which Norman functions and which Richler does not succeed in effectively synchronizing: as a political character who eventually comes to postulate the advantages of traditional values over ideological solutions, and as an individual troubled by contradictions and ambivalent feelings, who, like Noah, rejects one world without knowing exactly what is the alternative.

Richler's depiction of Winkleman's coterie and of Ernst is affected as well by his political thesis that the North American refugees were concerned more with power than with principles. The Americans are not given as full or as balanced a portrait as is Ernst. Aside from their politics, Richler reveals little else of their lives and stresses their generic qualities rather than their individuality. He briefly mentions Bob Landis's amorous affairs and Winkleman's warm relationship with his wife but not pervasively enough to render them fully realized characters. Moreover, Richler tends to use pejorative images to describe them when they are together: "a puddle of theatrical people"; "Winkleman floated drowsily . . . like a whale among smaller fish"; "Winkleman and others made deals and entered into publicised secret partnerships only to keep in practice, like generals disputing imaginary deads in a battle exercise" (27–29). By pitting this group of faceless characters against a more fully realized Ernst, Richler makes it easy for the reader to condemn them, but, at the same time, he casts doubts on his objective handling of the moral issue of the novel, and perhaps can be accused of thematic slovenliness.

In his portrayal of Ernst, Richler strives to introduce various facets of his character that counterbalance his evident ruthlessness. In so doing, Richler renders Ernst's thematic function clear; he has to have redeeming qualities to spur Norman on to challenge the morality of the American émigrés. This contrapuntal characterization of Ernst is too contrived. Richler evidently views Ernst as ambivalently as he does Ernst's more maturely realized version, Duddy Kravitz, but his counterpointing portrait of the latter is more organic. In Ernst's case the compensatory aspects of his character and situation, not much different from Duddy's, are introduced too factitiously: his father suffered at the hands of both the Nazis and the communists; his murder of Nicky is unintentional; he nurses sick drunks on the streets of Paris; he is a gifted singer but modestly hides his talent; a victim of harsh circumstances from birth, he wistfully listens to Sally talk of her happy childhood; and he quickly develops a romanticism that occasionally overlays his deep-seated cynicism.

Ernst, like Norman, is defined primarily by his political outlook. He has learnt quite early the futility of hoping for betterment through political creeds for they have all betrayed him. This knowledge has made him opportunistic and selfish, not wise and tolerant like Chaim. He is set on surviving at any cost even if he has to kill, and he cynically rejects Norman's belief in "such things . . . as dignity, honour, and love" (185), openly admitting to being unprincipled and espousing amorality: "There is no right or wrong. There are conditions, rewards, punishments, and sides, but that's all" (108). His disillusionment with communism began on learning of his father's ironical experience. His father was sent to prison for objecting to Hitler during the Nazi regime and after the war was imprisoned by the communists. The communist official turned out to be the same one who had questioned him for the Nazis, and the cell in which the communists put him was an old Gestapo cell.

Richler burdens Ernst's characterization also with the metaphorical function of underlining that basically all men are Jews. Like Kraus of *The Acrobats,* Ernst is without a country and continuously persecuted. He himself recognizes the Jewishness of his predicament: "It's almost like I was a Jew myself . . ." (160). Richler deliberately parallels Norman's account of the heroism of Hornstein, a Jew in the RCAF,

with Ernst's rescue of Hyman Gordon in Montreal. To win acceptance by his gentile colleagues in the RCAF, even if it has to be post-
humous, Horstein chose to stay with his plunging aircraft, piloting
it away from a populated area although he could have bailed out.
Similarly, Ernst, wanting desperately to be accepted, is willing to
sacrifice his life to save someone who spurns him.

Richler's employment of his principal characters both to prove his
political thesis and to explore their individual experiences weakens his
presentation of the triangular love affair of Sally, Norman, and Ernst.
Too often the lovers' actions and conversations are dictated more by
the requirements of the political theme than by any psychological
truth in characterization. Norman, for instance, initially resents Ernst
as a rival for Sally's love yet he obtains an invitation for Ernst and
Sally to Winkleman's party where he knows Ernst will not be wel-
comed. Perhaps Norman's action is intended to show he is mature
enough to overcome his resentment of Ernst and offer him a helping
hand, but this is not convincingly shown. When Sally first meets
Norman she responds to him on the political level, perceiving him
and his friends as frauds who, unlike her father, do not measure up
to the socialist ideals. Norman and Sally's subsequent attraction to
each other seems fabricated. Like Richler's other female characters,
Sally is all surface. Her importance is primarily to bring about the
meeting of Ernst and Norman, and once this is accomplished she is
removed by a convenient, melodramatic suicide. In *Joshua Then and
Now* Richler relates a similar triangular affair (involving Joshua,
Colin Fraser, a self-proclaimed communist, and his wife Pauline)
which is far more successfully handled, primarily because Richler allows the characters a life of their own instead of enslaving them to
his thesis.

One of Richler's fortes, evident in his early novels, is his keen perception of losers like Barney of *The Acrobats* and Charlie of *A Choice
of Enemies*. Charlie is perhaps the most psychologically credible character. On the periphery of Winkleman's group, he functions mini-
mally in Richler's study of Norman's relationship with the two
antithetical sets of refugees. Charlie does help to underline the
immorality of the American colony: he betrays Norman and, arriving
in London at the same time as Ernst, is tolerated by Winkleman's
coterie because of his political persuasion while Ernst is rejected. But
Charlie has an existence of his own apart from Richler's account of
the political antagonisms, and this is largely responsible for the
strength of his characterization.

When he first appears in the novel, he has come with Joey to make a fresh start in London, and though middle-aged, he exudes youthful enthusiasm and optimism. Like Friar of *The Apprenticeship of Duddy Kravitz,* he falsely claims to be a victim of McCarthy's committee as an excuse for his failure as a scriptwriter in North America. Throughout the novel, he both acknowledges and denies that he is a loser, refusing to relinquish his youthful yearning for success and fame. His wife, more realistic and practical, allows Charlie his pipe dreams until the climactic scene where, drunk and resentful that Norman is their benefactor, she forces Norman to reveal that it was his revision of Charlie's poor script that persuaded Winkleman to accept it. This confrontation with Norman leads to a poignant reconciliation between Charlie and his wife when both acknowledge their vulnerability and need for each other. Several such scenes bespeak Charlie's fragility and persuade the reader to retain sympathy for him despite his betrayal of Norman. Moreover, he experiences remorse though typically he takes no action to assuage his pricks of conscience. Unlike Ernst, his redeeming qualities are not mechanically imposed on him. His faults and his virtues are integrally and organically part of his psyche.

Published between *Son of a Smaller Hero* and *The Apprenticeship of Duddy Kravitz,* Richler's novels set in the Montreal ghetto and peopled by Jewish characters, *A Choice of Enemies* surprisingly has few Jewish characters and concerns. The main figures, Norman, Sally, Ernst, and most of the minor characters are not Jewish. Winkleman is, and there is a suggestion that his coterie is primarily Jewish, but political rather than ethnic matters bind them together. Winkleman at one point does reject Ernst because of atavistic resentment, and Charlie feels that he would be more readily accepted by the group were he Jewish. But these aspects are raised only incidentally. Karp is Jewish, but though Richler passingly mentions his experience in a concentration camp, he uses his Jewishness to establish the ironic parallels between his and Ernst's experiences, for despite their racial origin, both are kindred spirits, frighteningly alone and set on surviving at any cost.

Though Richler does not include extensive description of setting as he does in the two earlier novels, *The Acrobats* and *Son of a Smaller Hero,* he captures vividly the sense of place, particularly of the two districts where the émigrés live: Swiss Cottage and Hampstead. The setting is conveyed primarily through the consciousness of the principal characters, Norman, Ernst, and Sally, and in doing so Richler effectively evokes their constant sense of being, as Norman says, "aliens" (132) in London. Unlike Noah Adler who instinctively knows his Montreal and absorbs it through all the senses, Norman, Ernst, and Sally are almost always portrayed standing back and observing rather than becoming part of the London setting: "Norman turned up Church Street. There he saw a pretty girl with a furled umbrella waiting at the bus stop" (5); Sally "descended into the Heath proper and counted all the boys with scarves and all the girls who wore glasses" (111); and "Ernst was immediately struck by the brutalised faces of the spivs and whores who worked the different corners" (114).

The novel has, like all of the early novels, a straightfoward, chronological structural frame. Within this, however, Richler often juxtaposes for emphasis accounts of the antithetical societies to which the principal characters are exposed. Ernst's and Charlie's initial experiences in London and with the Winkleman crowd are placed next to each other in Chapters 4 and 5 of Part 2. And scenes of Norman's relationship with the North American émigrés and with Ernst virtually alternate in the second and third parts. The loose structure of the novel is accentuated in the last two parts by two characteristically Richlerian digressive scenes. In one, which describes a Canadian television program, Richler pokes fun at Canada's cultural provincialism, using Charlie as his prime satirical target even though this is markedly inconsistent with his sympathetic treatment of Charlie elsewhere in the novel. In the second set scene Richler introduces Morley Scott-Hardy, a homosexual critic, and his partner, Pip, two characters who seem to have sprung from the music hall or vaudeville. They are tenuously linked to the main narrative since they provide Norman with lodgings during his spell of amnesia. But Richler's extended account of their solitary appearance in the novel is evidently satirical in function. The targets of Richler's satire are literary and cultural pretensions: Scott-Hardy, for instance, tells Norman of a seance he held in which Henry James made an appearance: "I asked James if he was the protagonist of *The American,* and he replied 'Tut-tut, young man.' I thought that was frightfully clever" (167).

A Choice of Enemies is an improvement on Richler's first two novels. However, it is not a work that, as one critic suggests, marks the end of "the apprenticeship of Mordecai Richler,"[21] primarily because Richler too obviously manipulates narrative and character development to serve his particular thesis. This manipulation prevents Norman from becoming as fully realized and as convincing a character as

Jake Hersh of *St. Urbain's Horseman* who is similar in age and temperament. In this later novel, as in *The Apprenticeship of Duddy Kravitz* and *Joshua Then and Now,* Richler's more mature works, the author takes particular care to allow the theme to emerge organically from, rather than constrict, the natural evolution of the narrative and the protagonists.[22]

Chapter Four
The Humorous Novels:
The Incomparable Atuk
and *Cocksure*

Between the publication of *The Apprenticeship of Duddy Kravitz* (1959) and *St. Urbain's Horseman* (1971), Richler, kept busy with journalism and screen scripts, produced just two novels, *The Incomparable Atuk* and *Cocksure*. These strikingly similar novels mark a departure from the more or less sober realism of the earlier works. Dispensing altogether with any consideration of credibility and utilizing exaggerated characterization and fantastic plotting, they prominently display Richler's considerable talent for sustained humor, of which the preceding novels have hinted in several set scenes. In both novels the predominant form of narration is the dramatic, and the pervasive, brisk dialogue plainly reflects Richler's parallel involvement at this time with film and television scripts. Both novels accent the storytelling technique of suspense, which increasingly becomes a mark of Richler's plotting in his later works. And in both novels, particularly in *Cocksure,* there are many instances of Richler's ambivalence tempering the cogency of any sustained satirical rebukes and rendering ambiguous the function of his humor.

The Incomparable Atuk

The Incomparable Atuk or *Stick Your Neck Out* (the title of the American edition) is Richler's shortest novel, but despite its slightness, it is adroitly plotted and overflowing with zestful caricatures of the fraudulent and the affected drawn from the social and cultural circles of Toronto of the 1950s. Richler utterly disregards the element of probability in formulating the central idea of the novel which tells of the picaresque adventures of Atuk, an Eskimo poet. When the novel opens, Atuk is living in the Canadian Arctic where he is discovered by Rory Peel, an advertising executive, who sees in Atuk's poetry promotional possibilities for one of his clients, Twentyman Fur Company. Peel makes Atuk his protégé, gets his poetry published in a number of advertisements and later in a book, and eventually brings the now-celebrated poet to Toronto where he becomes the major attraction at literary parties, coffeehouses, and television shows. On these occasions he meets a number of social and cultural figures including television personalities, newspaper columnists, religious leaders, university professors, and sports champions, with whom he establishes various relationships that provide some hilarious situations.

In many of these situations Atuk functions initially as an artless figure whose primitive innocence serves to undercut the pretensions of civilized society. But it becomes apparent quite early in the novel that Richler does not portray him solely as a romantic innocent. He is shown to be no better than those around him. His artlessness is a mask cunningly cultivated to improve his social and financial status. He deliberately writes simplistic verse and rubs noses instead of shaking hands because this is what his admirers expect of him. Within a few months of his arrival in Toronto his materialistic and exploitative nature surfaces when he imprisons his trusting relatives in a Toronto basement to mass-produce pieces of Eskimo sculpture, the profit from the sale of which he keeps for himself.

Atuk's dubious career as businessman-artist comes to an abrupt end with his macabre death on Twentyman's television quiz show. Richler's account of this final episode of the novel, which is the resolution of what could be considered the main plot, illustrates clearly how both farfetched and intricate is the narrative. Buck Twentyman, the Canadian business tycoon, whose financial empire includes pulp and paper factories, fur companies, breweries, department stores, and commercial television, has obtained a large Chinese order for tractors, which he is likely to lose because of American pressure on Canadian trade with Communist China. To overcome this coercion from the United States, Twentyman and his executives conspire to exploit Atuk and Canadian nationalism on a television show, *Stick Out Your Neck,* sponsored by Twentyman. At this time, Atuk has been arrested for a pre-novel act of cannibalism on a United States Air Force colonel in the Arctic, and Twentyman, through his newspapers and television companies, uses Atuk's arrest to whip up anti-American feelings, urging the Canadian populace not to allow the beloved Eskimo poet to be punished just to please the Americans. Soon mobs begin to demonstrate in the streets, and, at this opportune moment, Twentyman chooses Atuk as the first contestant for his unique quiz show on which the guillotine is the penalty for failing to answer questions. He then secretly sells his program to an American sponsor. Atuk is decapitated, having been betrayed by Twentyman who promised to flash him the answers on cue cards. On learning who sponsored the show which caused the death of their beloved indigenous poet, the crowds rage against the United States. The anti-American feeling is so strong that at the end of the novel Twentyman is virtually assured the success of his deal with China.

Many of the characters Atuk meets on his picaresque journey through Toronto's social world have episodes to themselves that are as farfetched as the main plot, to which, though often only tangentially related, they impart further complication. There are, for instance, episodes which tell of Sergeant Jock Wilson of the Royal Canadian Mounted Police winning the Miss Canada beauty contest; of Seymour Bone becoming a famous theater critic when his hasty departure from a play because of overeating is misinterpreted as an angry reaction to the play; of the prejudiced Panofsky, disguised as a physician, switching babies at a Protestant hospital for eighteen years to prove that gentile children are all alike and interchangeable; of Bette Dolan, a champion long-distance swimmer and national heroine, becoming a nymphomaniac after her seduction by the wily Atuk; of Rory Peel screaming in his fall-out shelter, having been locked in by his German maid whom he employs to show that he is not a prejudiced Jew.

In addition to these zany episodes, Richler includes many briefer sketches which offer brilliant caricatures of figures like Doc Park, the physical education specialist, who is "world-famous . . . all over Canada";[1] Harry Snipes, a fiercely nationalistic editor, who plagiarizes stories from American magazines; Fr. McKendrick who proudly "told the rabbi about an enterprising priest in Victoria who had worked out a special deal with the local shopping plaza, and how he now gave away trading stamps in the confession box" (127); Professor Gore, the professional liberal, who is most solicitous about minorities as long as they remain true to his stereotyped conception of them; and Ruthy Bone, a caricature of the more realistically portrayed Jenny of *St. Urbain's Horseman,* who marries a literary critic instead of a dentist to prove she is not ghetto-bound.

These caricatures tend to absorb the reader, but, fascinating as they are, they never completely distract him from the narrative, which is made more engrossing by Richler's adherence to the technique of suspense in structuring the novel. Richler continuously arouses curiosity about what happens next and how the pieces fall into place. From the opening page he invites speculation about the nature of the dreadful equipment Twentyman is unloading and does not provide the answer until the last chapter. Other mysteries appear every so often throughout the novel: What heinous crime did Atuk commit? What is the nature of Panofsky's research which requires him to masquerade as Dr. Zale in the maternity ward of the Protestant Temperance Hospital? What is the game show *Stick Out Your Neck* all about? Why were the couple in the park so flustered when Rory Peel turned to look at them? In this slight novel this element of suspense is not accented as much as it is in Richler's more substantial works like *Joshua Then and Now;* nevertheless, it is quite cleverly done and, together with the engaging plot and witty caricatures, makes *The Incomparable Atuk* a very entertaining piece.

A major critical question posed by the novel, which has elicited opposite responses from George Woodcock and Malcolm Ross, is what exactly is Richler's attitude or tone to the Toronto social scene? While Woodcock feels that "light satire is perhaps the best term to describe this amusing but insubstantial book,"[2] Ross believes that the "comedy is as black as it is brilliant. There is hard, even cruel mockery in Richler's laughter."[3] Certain critics find it less easy to take a firm stand on the nature of Richler's intent. F. W. Watt, for example, wonders about Richler's view of his characters, "with what gravity does he offer it and do we receive it?"[4] And Granville Hicks, having observed that "Richler lets his satire range freely," adds: "Often enough satire becomes farce."[5] In his essays and articles Richler tends to criticize harshly the pretentious Canadian cultural groups of the 1950s, and it is quite possible that he is doing that here as well; but he is also having fun. He himself has described the novel as "a much gentler book [than *Cocksure*]. More of a spoof."[6] Whatever was his conscious intent when he wrote the novel, various stylistic and technical aspects work against it being a sustained satirical piece.

In the first instance, the situation and characters, though plainly fascinating, are too extravagant, too wildly implausible to be successful satirical put-downs. Satire depends on exaggeration, even grotesque exaggeration, but when the original is completely distorted, the object satirized is lost sight of, and the distortion begins to exist on its own and not as a satirical reflection. This is what happens with

Richler's characterization and plotting. An obvious example is the extended account of Atuk's decapitation on the outlandish television
show where Richler becomes more absorbed with his bizarre plotting
than with satiric rebuke. Another is the portrayal of Sergeant Wilson
of the RCMP, through whom Richler initially appears to be satiriz-
ing inept and officious policemen. The satire, however, gives way to
farce in the scenes of mistaken identity where Wilson and McEwan,
a crusading newspaper columnist, both of whom are masquerading as
their opposite sex, fall in love. Taking this situation to its most unlikely extreme, Richler tells of Wilson, in his disguise as a woman,
winning the Miss Canada crown with the help of McEwan, and preparing, on orders from his superiors, for the Miss Universe contest.

If there is a central issue in the novel, it is (as Richler's use as an
epigraph of a quotation from the American writer, Richard Rovere,
suggests) Canada's narrow nationalism which creates an insularity
that seeks to exclude all outside influence, particularly American, and
fosters the parochial celebrity who is "world-famous . . . all over
Canada." Richler assembles a large number of characters to allow him
to touch on many aspects of this issue: politics, religion, industry and
commerce, education, sports, the media, the performing arts, literature, race relations, and sexual mores. But the consequences of such
a colorful but broad spectrum are that Richler spreads himself too
thinly in so slim a volume, and whatever satire was intended loses its
intensity. Intensity diminishes too because Richler bears down too
much on the superficial and the obvious: Seymour Bone's ability as a
critic, for instance, is subjected to brief jibes, but there is no keen
ironical perception and the exact nature of his critical deficiencies is
not examined. Richler appears to be content in this novel to provide
farcical diversions rather than arresting revelations on human
conduct.

Richler's characterization of Atuk encourages the reader to respond
to the novel as farce. Perhaps had he portrayed Atuk consistently as
an *ingénu* whose artless perceptions strip away the pretenses of the
Torontonians, the work would have had a stronger satiric tone; but
given Atuk's own corrupt nature, when he appears in scenes with
members of the civilized society, the reader enjoys the conflict of villain against villain, and does not bother to determine who is in fact
the true savage. A few critics consider Atuk to be "an Eskimo version
of Duddy."[7] In his relentless amoral struggle to achieve success in a
materialistic world, he certainly is a skeletal parallel to Duddy, but

he does not engage the reader's feeling nor does he elicit an ambivalent response from the author as does Duddy. Richler presents Atuk quite clearly as a caricature whose primary function is to provide amusement for the reader.

There are some scenes of black humor which have satirical potential; the satire, however, is dissipated by the juxtaposition of these scenes with unambiguously farcical episodes. Atuk deliberately sending Mush Mush, a relative he exploits in his sweatshop, to his death by telling him to cross a street against the traffic light, can be taken as an instance of Atuk's cold abuse of his people. But this incident occurs immediately after the utterly zany scene in McEwan's office where Mush Mush, after examining McEwan's head and stomach, pronounces that she is not a white woman, using as his criterion a television commercial which shows in animated form how aspirin affects the head and stomach of a woman. Is Mush Mush's death just a continuation of this farcical tone? In which case, is Atuk free from blame since Mush Mush is little more than a Disney-animated figure who will spring back to life after his accident which is contrived for its humorous effect? Richler's presentation of the ridiculous television program "Crossed Swords" through the eyes of a viewer, Bette Dolan, as she awaits with mounting sensuality the arrival of Atuk in her apartment, similarly renders ambiguous the satire on the posturing television personalities who are unable to identify the quotation, "Blessed are the meek: for they shall inherit the earth" (90).

Two scenes retain some satirical force mainly because of the particular technique Richler employs in each. Both, however, could quite conceivably be more firmly satirical were they removed from the novel's tempering farcical context. The first is Professor Gore's televised annual dinner, where are gathered all the cultural and social charlatans of the novel. This crowd scene, filled with airs and pretensions, is rich with satiric possibilities. Richler presents the scene mainly through the eyes of the television camera and quite effectively employs the cinematic montage to shift rapidly from one affected group to another, and, more important, to sharpen the satire on characters who, aware of the television cameras, exaggerate their behavior, thus unwittingly parodying and caricaturing themselves.

Atuk's conflict with his father and Rory Peel over his proposed mixed marriage with Goldie Panofsky is perhaps one of the less ambiguously satirical episodes. This is essentially because of Richler's effective use of satirical allegory. In Atuk's relationship with others his Eskimo identity is fairly intact, but when he confronts his father, the Old One, with the question of his marriage outside his race, Richler transforms him into an allegorical reflection of a Jew who comes up against the traditional Jewish attitude to mixed marriages. The allegory is underlined by recurring expressions that evoke Jewish experiences: "igloo mentality" (83); "we are the chosen pagans" (86); "For an Eskimo boy to make his mark in this world, Atuk, he must be brighter, better, and faster than other boys" (53); "I am a man who just happens to be an Eskimo" (84).[8] When Peel objects to Atuk's marriage to his sister, the Eskimo's response is charged with Jewish connotations:

> "To hell with it. I will not apologize for what I am. He could have called me anything but an 'aggressive Eskimo.' " Atuk blew his nose. "When I used to ski to school as a kid the white boys used to knock me over and beat me up and call me a dirty Eskimo."
> "Oh, my poor darling."
> "I have feelings too, you know. If you prick me, do I not bleed?" (117)

Even before the echo of Shakespeare's Shylock, the passage convinces of Richler's allegorical intention. The technique of using one race to explore the shortcomings of another, which Richler employs even more sophisticatedly in his account of Mortimer Griffin's relationship with Shalinsky in *Cocksure*, serves to place the issues in a fresh context and to strip away from them the veil of familiarity which reconciles the individual to them and prevents him from seeing them as they really are.

In an early observation on young British writers Richler stated that they "seem to be writing almost provincial undergraduate jokes in a very special context."[9] To a large extent, this comment is applicable to the author of *The Incomparable Atuk* for he seldom takes himself too seriously and chooses to focus on provincial rather than larger issues. While Canadian reviewers cheerily speculated about the real-life counterparts of Richler's caricatures, an American reviewer was "mystified by what are obviously inside jokes to 'hip' Canadians."[10] The novel is cocooned in Canada, or more precisely Toronto of the fifties, and it certainly lacks the wider scope of the later *Cocksure;* but it should not be faulted for not being what it never was intended to be. *The Incomparable Atuk,* though not a potboiler, is certainly a *jeu d'esprit,* occupying a special position in Richler's *oeuvre*.

Cocksure

Cocksure has the extravagant plotting and fantastic characterization of *The Incomparable Atuk,* but it is quite evidently neither as parochial nor as frivolous as the earlier novel. Though it focuses on the misadventures of a Canadian innocent in swinging London of the 1960s, it is not primarily concerned with Canadian issues. The novel looks inclusively at the ubiquitous decline of spiritual values and moral responsibility in contemporary society at large. Richler is angered, not amused, by the forces generating this decline. Consequently, the humor here is more militant, the imagery more grotesque, and the language more ribald than in *The Incomparable Atuk.* The ribaldry and grotesquerie, which some interpreted as obscenity, were responsible for the mild sensation the novel occasioned on publication: W. H. Smith bookstores in Britain refused to stock it, and Australia, New Zealand, and South Africa banned it altogether.

One aspect of *Cocksure's* inclusiveness is its broad depiction of the protagonist, Mortimer Griffin, in three contiguous spheres of activity. Mortimer appears as a man of affairs, as a member of a particular ethnic group, and as a family man. Each sphere has a distinct narrative strand to itself. Richler quite skillfully weaves these various strands together through a common emphasis on grotesque images, extravagant situations, and bizarre characters. Mortimer, who features in every episode of the novel, is himself an important unifying device.

The narrative which traces Mortimer's experiences as a man of affairs describes his confrontation with the dreaded Star Maker. When the novel opens, Mortimer has a fairly secure job as a senior editor in a prestigious London publishing house, Oriole Press. He is on the verge of becoming its director, when the Star Maker, a Hollywood super-tycoon, buys Oriole Press to extend his vast film and publishing empire. The new owner initiates a series of biographies on contemporary personalities. Mortimer discovers to his detriment that the Star Maker ensures the success of this series by arranging the death of the subject of each biography in sensational circumstances just before publication. Mortimer is hunted by the Star Maker's assassins to prevent him from divulging this appalling trade secret, and the novel ends with him preparing for his inevitable death at their hands. The second narrative relates Mortimer's persecution by Shalinsky, the editor of *Jewish Thought.* Mortimer is Anglo-Canadian, but Shalinsky perversely insists that he is denying his Jewish identity. Mortimer's friends, believing Shalinsky despite Mortimer's protests, dub him a racist and ostracize him. The third parallel narrative follows the triangular relationship among Mortimer, his wife Joyce, and his best friend Ziggy. Joyce has an open affair with Ziggy. Tormented by this, Mortimer seeks out other women who serve only to increase his sense of inadequacy and inferiority.

These narratives, informed by the principle of *reductio ad absurdum* rather than by any thought to credibility, are rich in fantastic characters and incidents. Richler summons up episodes which tell of the Star Maker, composed of transplanted organs and limbs, deliberately making himself androgynous and impregnating himself; of movie stars created by literally inflating rubber models which are deflated and stored away until required; of the eccentric benevolence of Lord Woodcock for Nazi war criminals; of Hy Rosen, a diminutive avenging Jew, who accosts innocent strangers in the streets with accusations of anti-Semitism before vengefully punching them in the stomach; of Mortimer's young son's education at a permissive school, the Beatrice Webb House, where ten-year-olds perform De Sade's *Philosophy in the Bedroom* nude on stage; of a pious schoolteacher, Miss Ryerson, resorting to fellatio as a form of reward for good students; of Ziggy's avant-garde film which celebrates everything abnormal; of the ridicule of Mortimer's Victoria Cross on an inane talk show; of the intrusion of politics and racism in Mortimer's abortive sexual relationship with Rachel Coleman, a black librarian at Oriole Press; and of Polly Morgan living life cinematically with cuts and fade-outs.

George Woodcock, commenting on Richler's involved plotting, argues that the novel progresses along "two currents of action—deriving from the Star Maker and from Shalinsky—that never really coalesce," and that the imagery and themes underline this lack of cohesion because the Star Maker narrative, unlike the rest of the novel, is peopled by fantastic and grotesque characters that are barely flesh and blood, and because it focuses on the evils of modern life while the Shalinsky level concentrates on follies. Though it is true that one current of action is more grisly and grotesque than the other, Woodcock's conclusion that there is "no real fusion"[11] between the two is not wholly justified. To begin with, Richler, who is exploring Mortimer's experiences as a professional, as a member of his race, and as a family man, employs at least one other current of action to tell of Mortimer's relationship with his wife and Ziggy, on which impinges

Mortimer's involvement with the resourceful chemist, Rapani, with Rachel Coleman, with Miss Ryerson and the Beatrice Webb House, and with Polly Morgan. Most of these episodes could hardly be attached even tenuously to either the Star Maker or the Shalinsky level. The Star Maker narrative is certainly more prominent than the other two; however, it is a prominence achieved through Richler's use of this narrative (with which *Cocksure* begins and ends) to give the novel its structural frame, and not through any spatial emphasis since Richler allots equal space to the three spheres of Mortimer's life.

The Star Maker is indeed a repulsive, nauseating, obscene, Tiresias figure, whose self-impregnation is the perfect satirical image of the narcissistic tycoon who plays god with the lives of his underlings. Equally fantastic, but more fanciful than grotesque, are the images of the Star Maker's actors who hang limply in closets when not needed to act in films. Such grotesque and fantastic images are not restricted to the Star Maker episodes, however. In the parallel narratives there are the grotesque accounts of Ziggy's girl drinking with relish his urine from a pint-sized beer mug; of the nauseating ring-a-ding sentimental barbecue of Treblinka; of the repulsive black maggoty clumps infesting Joyce's armpits; of the ribald performance of De Sade's *Philosophy in the Bedroom* by lisping fledglings; of the pious and proper Miss Ryerson resorting to fellating her young students, which certainly demands a suspension of disbelief equal to that required by the image of rubberized actors. Grotesqueries emanating from the novel's ubiquitous use of raw, coarse language and from the dominant technique of *reductio ad absurdum* appear in all spheres of Mortimer's activities.

Vices certainly are present in the Star Maker episodes, as Woodcock observes. Richler satirizes the Star Maker's vicious, cannibalistic exploitation of his underlings and his callous disregard for human life in achieving commercial success. But he also pokes fun at a frivolous target: in long-drawn-out episodes, one of which describes a rough-and-tumble chase, he shows actors to be nothing more than vacuous rubberized robots—going one step further than the movie director Josef Von Sternberg who sees them as puppets. The other narrative levels censure vices as well as foibles. Ziggy, who is as irretrievably immoral as the Star Maker, blackmails homosexuals from whom he has extracted love letters and impregnates "French Canadian girls, raising babies to the age of three months, and then selling them to childless couples in Manhattan."[12] The equally immoral Digby-Jones pillories a dedicated nun on his irreverent talk show, pronouncing that her activity among the poor is born of sexual frustration and describing her as *"a sexually diverted nymphomaniac"* (123).

To hold the reader's interest in a satirical work, Richler has observed, is a difficult task since protagonists in satires, who are as a rule not fully developed, do not easily engage the reader's sympathy. "It's much more arduous and of course much more cunning than if you were writing *St. Urbain's Horseman* or *Duddy Kravitz,* where the reader identifies . . . with the protagonist. You've got a lot more going for you, and it's not so difficult to keep the reader's attention when you have that."[13] In *Cocksure,* having to forego the reader's easy identification with the protagonist, Richler once more employs the ageless storytelling technique of suspense. The novel is constructed in a straightforward, episodic manner but the episodes are arranged in such a way that the reader is constantly induced to wonder what happens next and what bearing a particular incident has on another.

In the first chapter, for instance, Richler takes hold of the reader with some puzzling and mysterious incidents: Who and what are the Star Maker's spare-parts men, and why does the terrified Tomasso pretend to have difficulty with the eye chart? Why is the Star Maker linked with the legendary and historical hermaphrodites Tiresias and Chevalier d'Éon? Why does Tomasso get off scot-free after uttering rash, otherwise unforgivable, profanities to the Star Maker? What could the account of the Star hanging in a closet possibly mean? Why does Tomasso feel in his bones that Mortimer is going to cause him trouble? As the answers to some of these questions gradually unfold, others are progressively added: Why is Mortimer so secretive about his war record? And again, why so secretive about the contents of his cupboard? Why does the biography series require the services of the uniformed efficiency team from Frankfurt? These incremental mysteries prompt the reader to go on and give this fast-paced novel added impetus.

Written nine years after *The Apprenticeship of Duddy Kravitz,* during which time Richler was kept busy with film and television scripts, *Cocksure,* like *The Incomparable Atuk,* invites analysis in cinematic terms. The pervasive dialogue, at times contributing incrementally to the narrative, at others exploding with appealing wit and humor, could so easily have been lifted from a film script. The montage, cuts, and dissolves (seen, for instance, in the transitional fading-out and fading-in on Tomasso's thick pebble glasses at the end of Chapter

Twelve and the beginning of Chapter Thirteen) all contribute to the thriller tempo of the main narrative. The James Bond movies were at their peak of popularity when *Cocksure* was published in 1968, the year, incidentally, that Richler published an article censuring the xenophobia of the Bond novels.[14] The opening scene of *Cocksure* recalls and probably parodies the pre-credit opening of the Bond movies: the camera picks up Tomasso's AC Cobra 427 driving up to a wrought-iron gate, follows it past guards, through a cypress-lined driveway, to a swimming pool graced by a bikini-clad nurse. There is a cut to Tomasso approaching a figure in a wheelchair—the dread Star Maker, who sends a reluctant Tomasso on a mission to London. There is another cut to Tomasso on a plane to London, and as he picks up Mortimer's photograph, of which the camera gives a close-up, the credits appear, at the end of which Mortimer's photographic image fades out and Mortimer himself, listening with Miss Ryerson to a soapboxer in Hyde Park (Chapter 2 of the novel) fades in. *Cocksure* abounds with such parallels to film scripts, and these make the novel perhaps the one most easily adaptable to the screen. In fact, among Richler's papers at the University of Calgary, there are several drafts and manuscripts of television and radio versions of certain scenes, such as Mortimer's conflict with Shalinsky and his relationship with Hy Rosen and Joyce, that are just slightly different from their counterparts in the novel.

Mortimer's principal function in the novel is as a satiric *ingénu*. However, though in this role he is more successful than Atuk, whose innocence is questioned from the beginning, he is not consistently portrayed as such. Richler gives him too complex an inner life (which perhaps is the consequence of his dependence on the early short-story version of the Mortimer-Shalinsky affair[15] where Mortimer is a fairly full-fledged character, realistically portrayed), and in his depiction of this inner life, Mortimer becomes a victim of doubts and conflicts. Like most of Richler's protagonists, he believes "in the possibilities within each of us for goodness" (221) and is genuinely disgusted with the depraved behavior around him, yet he often resents himself for what he stands for: "The virtues I was raised to believe in have become pernicious. Contemporary writing, he thought, is clawing at my balls, making me repugnant to myself. An eyesore" (102). He belittles himself for being hardworking, honest, and liberal, and appears to want admission to the society he condemns but is foiled by his moral upbringing. His abortive sexual adventures underline this desire; so do his initial defense of Ziggy's language, his admiration for Ziggy's expertise with women, and his envy of Ziggy's artistic talents. However, despite his flirting with this world, Mortimer remains on the outside, and it would appear that Philip Toynbee is overstating the case against him when he says that he "is not a Candide who is punished by the wicked world for his innocence, but simply a weaker member of the wicked world."[16]

Richler himself responds ambivalently to Mortimer's doubts and hesitations. He often shows him to be feckless, bumbling, and more naive than innocent; and he pokes fun at him. Yet he is clearly on Mortimer's side when Mortimer is up against the corrupt society. In fact, occasionally evident beneath the amusing portrayal is Richler's awareness of Mortimer's sad lot, as in the scene where Joyce is in bed with Ziggy in Mortimer's bedroom, while outside in the kitchen the overwrought Mortimer tries, in the company of his eight-year-old son, to come to terms with her infidelity; and at the end of the novel where Mortimer, abandoned by everyone, is unwittingly betrayed by a wistful Polly Morgan who, instead of fetching the police to save him from the Star Maker's killers, fades into her make-believe life on the silver screen. These are very likely some of the scenes that persuaded Desmond Pacey to say that he found the work "pathetic rather than comic."[17]

Allowing Mortimer a rich inner life and emotional involvement with other characters works against his role as a satiric *ingénu,* who as a rule acquires functionary strength by being dry and one-dimensional, as Richler himself has stated,[18] and by being on the periphery of the action, observing more than participating. Mortimer's conflicts and involved relationships either tend to distract the reader or come between him and the matter satirized. Richler's ambivalent portrayal of Mortimer further weakens his function as a satiric agent. His amusing account of Mortimer's immature obsession with his sexual potency during his affair with Rachel Coleman and Polly Morgan, and of his passive acceptance of the role of Casanova forced on him by Rapani's circle of lascivious old men, work against the satire on Ziggy's and Joyce's trendy morality.

Richler has mentioned that "the subject matter of *Cocksure* lent itself to savagery," and that the novel was written out of "disgust."[19] The work, however, though it is Richler's more pervasively satiric novel, never becomes a cogent, thoroughgoing satire. In fact, many of the early reviewers felt that Richler succeeds more in entertaining than in vexing the world. The work has been described as "a stylish farce" whose "absurdities are never truly disturbing"; as "smart-alecky stuff" that does not cut deeply; and as a "serio-comic novel" in which "Richler wears his jester's patches well."[20] An important reason for this critical response is, of course, Mortimer's failure as a consistent satiric *ingénu* and Richler's ambivalence toward him; but there are other causes.

The fascinating fast-paced narrative tends to shift the reader's attention away from the satire to itself. The inclusion of farcical scenes (such as those telling protractedly of Tamasso's apprehension for his eyes, Rapani and his cohorts pouring over torrid passages from Harold Robbins, Mortimer's quandary over the disposal of his stock of prophylactics, Polly's quirky behavior, and the slapstick chase of the Star in the studio) have a tempering effect on the satirical passages with which they are juxtaposed. Richler also includes, as the *Times Literary Supplement* reviewer observes, "more issues than it is competent to deal with, except facetiously."[21] He certainly confronts serious failings in society, but so rapidly is the reader wafted from one issue to another that he never is allowed to give his full attention to any. This becomes apparent when published extracts from the novel are read on their own. The account of the Beatrice Webb House teaching methods is an example. Published as a short story in *The Paris Review*, this piece has a satiric intensity not felt when it is read in the context of *Cocksure,* where, moreover, it is split into two nonsequential chapters (4 and 18) which further diffuses the satire.

Apart from its mellowing effect on the satire, Richler's ambivalent portrayal of Mortimer blurs and, for some critics, blots out completely the author's moral position. Philip Toynbee says that "a general weakness of this funny and memorable book is that it is quite impossible to detect the moral platform on which Mr. Richler is standing and from which his darts are launched."[22] Perhaps had Richler not whimsically abandoned his working title, "It's Harder to be Anybody," his moral stance would have been less elusive. Of his intention in writing the novel, Richler has stated that he was trying to see how far he "could make a case for that easily and glibly dismissed middle-class, decent, bill-paying, honourable man."[23] Despite the humor at Mortimer's expense, this intention remains evident in the novel. Richler sees Mortimer as the archetypal little man who though he may be unsure of himself and may occasionally wonder if the others are right and he is wrong, struggles to be himself and to live by traditional spiritual values in the face of constant persecution. Richler develops this theme in all three narrative spheres—which is a further aid to the structural cohesion of the novel. Mortimer's most obvious persecutor is the Star Maker, one of the truly grotesque satirical images in contemporary literature, a culmination of Kraus, Karp, Dingleman, and Twentyman. So utterly contemptible is he that Richler's moral position in this current of action is unambiguously clear. Richler condemns this callous, materialistic, and brutal exploiter who precipitates and lives off the misfortunes of others. Mortimer, at the cost of his life, refuses to be a part of his horrible empire.

In the domestic sphere of Mortimer's life his chief bane is Joyce's mindless trendiness. She indiscriminately espouses all liberal political causes, refusing, for instance, to buy vegetables imported from repressionist countries. Her humanitarian concern should certainly be exempt from satirical rebuke, but she is prompted, Richler makes clear, less by conviction than by a desire to be "thoroughly with it" (33). She knows all the popular phrases and which magazines and television shows are in vogue. Suspecting Mortimer of having a mistress gives her pleasure, for she finally has a modish husband. Her own affair with Ziggy is conducted according to the prevailing values: he will never marry her because he respects her too much. Like Aunt Ida of *The Apprenticeship of Duddy Kravitz,* she is very much a pseudo-Freudian, but, unlike Ida, she is more cogently satirized.

Joyce, not surprisingly, sends her son to the fashionable Beatrice Webb House, an ultraliberal institution modeled on Summerhill, which Richler zestfully attacks. Certain satirical scenes such as the lengthy classroom discussion of de Sade's sexuality, the nude stage play, and Miss Ryerson's unique way of rewarding students appear to be so extremely exaggerated and removed from the original target as to lose their satirical effectiveness. Any familiarity with the experimental approach to education at Summerhill, however, would suggest that Richler perhaps understates rather than overstates, for A. S. Neill, the Headmaster, has mentioned, for instance, that the concept of virginity convulses him with laughter and he sees nothing wrong with adolescents staging a love-in or a gang rape.[24] That Richler is firmly against such experimentation in education is quite clear, but to make the satire legitimate and effective, the question of Summerhill, which has been argued back and forth by educationists, deserves more detailed attention. Richler's treatment of this target tends to be superficial and entertaining rather than incisive and scathing.

Richler initially introduced silver-haired Miss Ryerson, Mortimer's fourth-grade teacher from Ontario, as a visitor to London who functions as a satiric *ingénue* censuring the deterioration of traditional values in swinging London. But this function dissipates quickly as Richler pokes fun at her sentimental colonial attachment and at her activities in Beatrice Webb House. Toynbee obviously has this inconsistent characterization of Miss Ryerson in mind also when he talks of Richler's elusive moral stance.

Ziggy, Joyce's lover, represents a set of values and a mode of life antithetical to Mortimer's. He has irretrievably rejected any form of morality and is ultimately more contemptible for directing his obvious talents and intelligence into perverse activities and for having no personal scruples. Richler satirizes his sexual perversion, his selfishness, and his faddish artistry. His film, *Different,* is included by Richler both as a satire on Ziggy's artistic pretensions and as an example of how Ziggy and his ilk persecute the conservative little man. Digby Jones, an obvious extension of Ziggy, mocks Mortimer for earning a Victoria Cross. Mortimer's heroism is more brutally treated by Jones and his audience than are Norman Price's acts of bravery by the wedding guests in *A Choice of Enemies.* Throughout the scene Richler allows Jones and his mob to ridicule themselves by their own comments, but at two points his anger overcomes him, forcing him to comment virtually directly. On the first occasion, Digby Jones's observation that a Victoria Cross winner once told him he enjoyed killing elicits this rebuke which has the ring of authorial intrusion: "In the ensuing laughter Mortimer noted that Dig had neglected to add that the captain in question had lost both his legs in the action for which he was decorated" (218). The second time Richler cannot refrain from sarcasm when responding to Digby's and his audience's mock sympathy for Mortimer the hero: "As Mortimer, followed by the camera, slunk offstage, nobody laughed. Nobody scoffed. He was not ridiculed. Swingers, after all, were not without pity" (223).

Perhaps the strongest evocation of the theme of the difficulty of being one's self in contemporary society is seen in Shalinsky's relentless persecution of Mortimer. In the short-story version of this narrative Mortimer is in fact half Jewish and is made fun of because of his denial of his Jewish parentage. He eventually marries Shalinsky's

daughter and espouses his father-in-law's way of life. In the novel,
however, Mortimer has no Jewish ancestry and reflects no anti-
Semitism; he compares favorably with his Jewish friend, Hy Rosen,
for it is Hy rather than Mortimer who exhibits embarrassment at his
parentage. Shalinsky's character also differs in the novel.

He is no
longer a likable, eccentric, intellectual and a considerate father, but
a merciless inquisitor through whom Richler satirizes, as he does less
extendedly in the parody of Virgil's magazine in *The Apprenticeship of
Duddy Kravitz,* the "tyranny of the minority" (205). Shalinsky's accusation of racial bias makes Mortimer, who previously has considered himself "refreshingly free from prejudice" (26), neurotically
concerned with how he relates to individuals of other races even when
he is making love. In a passage rich with mock rhetoric Mortimer
examines his motive for desiring Rachel Coleman: "Could it be, Mortimer thought, terrified, that this precious erection of his was im-
pure, not sexually motivated, but politically inspired . . . only a
lousy liberal gesture?" (179–80). Richler is making fun of Mortimer's
quandary in this scene, but the real butt of his satire is a society so
surfeited with prejudicial issues and so obsessed with sexual performance that it forces the innocent to indulge in unhealthy, gnawing
introspection.

Shalinsky's effort to force Mortimer into the Jewish mold is evidently an ironical device, but it demonstrates also Richler's tendency
to see Jews in the larger human context. Deserted by his wife, betrayed by his best friend, generally ostracized by his social group, and
pursued by the Star Maker's killers, Mortimer seeks refuge at Shalinsky's, where Shalinsky tells him that his experience of persecution
is characteristically Jewish, adding that a "Jew is an idea. Today you
are my idea of a Jew" (245). Given his characteristics, Shalinsky's
comment is quite ambiguous, for it is not clear whether at this point
he still sees Mortimer as a Jew in the racial or the metaphorical sense.
Richler, however, has the metaphorical interpretation in mind, as he
does when he makes Atuk echo Jewish expressions.

Richler's response to Germans and to the Nazi persecution of the
Jews is complex and can be discussed more profitably in relation to
St. Urbain's Horseman where it is an important theme. For the moment, it should be noted that Richler, intolerant of professional,
cause-hungry liberals, satirizes Lord Woodcock, the aging Fabian and
Mortimer's former employer, whose cause is playing down the Nazi
atrocities. Among the blackest pieces of Richler's militant humor is

his account of one of these atrocities. The mother of Lord Woodcock's Jewish secretary, Miss Fishman, who is admonished by her employer for her outbursts against Germans, was the millionth Jew to be burned at the ovens of Treblinka. It was a gala occasion, Richler mockingly reports, with festoons of flowers and gaily colored Chinese lanterns, "one of the most ring-a-ding nights in the history of the Third Reich, and to this day . . . it is commemorated by survivors of that sentimental barbecue wherever they may be" (40).

Satire is sometimes employed as a rhetorical device to hide a lack of incisive knowledge of endemic qualities of a society. Richler makes this point in an essay on his experiences with American writers in Paris during the 1950s: "the writer who opts out of the mainstream of American experience is . . . cutting himself off from his natural material, sacrificing his sense of social continuity; and so when we swung around to writing about contemporary America, we could only attack obliquely, shrewdly settling on a style that did not betray knowledge gaps of day to day experience."[25] It is very possible that satire is a rhetorical smokescreen in *The Incomparable Atuk,* as it is in Richler's portraits of certain gentile characters in other novels, but it is not predominantly so in *Cocksure,* for though in its finished form the novel reflects an ambivalent vision which weakens the satire, it is a work in which disgust and anger are still evident, and consequently constitutes Richler's firmest satirical expression so far.

Chapter Five
The Widening Scope:
St. Urbain's Horseman
and *Joshua Then and Now*

St. Urbain's Horseman and *Joshua Then and Now* are much more ambitiously conceived than the earlier novels. They have far more expansive geographical and temporal settings and examine a far wider range of experiences. They inclusively incorporate, and go beyond, the separate, restrictive settings of the earlier novels: the Montreal Jewish ghetto, the European émigré colonies, the Toronto social world, and swinging London of the sixties. The protagonists of the two novels are now middle-aged and have varied experiences as husbands, fathers, and sons, as artists and professionals, as social figures, and as individuals with particular ethnic and national allegiances. Moreover, both are obsessed—each for his own particular reasons—with reviewing their lives; consequently, numerous incidents and events from the distant and recent past are introduced. Many of these incidents and events have appeared before in the preceding novels, and their reappearance in *St. Urbain's Horseman* and *Joshua Then and Now* provides a fascinating opportunity for the reader to observe Richler's artistic development and his changing emphasis and perspective.

St. Urbain's Horseman: Narrative Structure

St. Urbain's Horseman is essentially a biographical study of a Jewish Canadian, Jake Hersh, who left Canada fourteen years earlier and now resides in London where he makes a living as a film director. The novel could be taken as a continuation of Noah Adler's story, beginning just about where *Son of a Smaller Hero* leaves off. Jake's biography is given additional narrative momentum by his imagined and actual quest for his footloose, adventurous cousin, Joey Hersh, known as the Horseman, and by Jake's trial at the Old Bailey for alleged rape, sodomy, indecent assault, and possession of cannabis. A host of minor plots and a gallery of characters impart to the novel an impression of narrative complexity. The novel gives an extended flashback to Jake's childhood primarily to introduce Joey and provide his background. Joey's mother, Hanna, abandoned by her irresponsible husband, lives with her children in a Montreal coldwater flat reluctantly provided by Uncle Abe, the patronizing head of the extended Hersh family. Joey resents Uncle Abe's charity and runs away from home. He returns as a strong and assertive man but soon leaves Montreal under mysterious circumstances, never to return home or to reappear in person in the novel. Certain members of the family, particularly Jake and Hanna, follow with keen interest his peregrination in various parts of the world. With his disappearance from the novel, the narrative shifts to Jake's experiences. As a young man, he joins the Canadian Broadcasting Corporation in Toronto, but though he eventually rises to the position of a film director, he feels culturally suffocated in Canada, and, scoffing at his homeland, he leaves for England with a friend, Luke Scott, a scriptwriter. In London, Luke becomes an acclaimed scriptwriter while Jake directs average films. After his marriage to Nancy, a gentile Canadian, he settles down to a fairly contented family life though he is perpetually conscious of Luke's success and his own mediocrity.

At this point Jake meets Ruthy, an Englishwoman whom the Horseman used and discarded some years earlier. Jake tries to make amends to her, and he eventually is introduced to her fiancé, Harry Stein, a vindictive little man who coincidentally works at the office of Jake's accountant. Harry implicates Jake in a sordid sex scandal. Allowed to use the Hershes' Hampstead home while Jake is attending his father's funeral in Montreal and the rest of the family is holidaying in Cornwall, Harry persuades a German *au pair* girl, Ingrid Loebner, to spend the night with him there. Jake returns home unexpectedly to find them indulging in various sexual games. Tired and irritable, he violently throws Ingrid out when she attempts to seduce him. As a result, Ingrid vengefully accuses Jake and Harry of rape for which they are charged, tried, and convicted though both are innocent. Jake is fined five hundred pounds while Harry is sent to prison. After the trial Jake learns that the Horseman was killed in Paraguay, either by Dr. Mengele, the Nazi war criminal, whom Jake believes he was hunting, or while involved in smuggling. At the end of the novel, Jake tries to rally himself after his traumatic court experience and the death of his beloved cousin, and appears to be picking up the pieces of his shattered life.

In organizing this extended and involved narrative, Richler chooses not to employ the chronological approach of his previous novels, adopting instead an intricate pattern of flashbacks within flashbacks. The current action of the novel extends just over a few days, beginning on the evening of the first day of Jake's appearance at the Old Bailey and ending a short while after the third and final day of the trial. Everything else is given in flashbacks. The novel is divided into four parts. Part 1 relates the incidents of the first evening and of the second day of the trial, with flashbacks to events in London, including Jake's first meeting with Nancy, and his more recent introduction to Ruthy and Harry. The second part is a major flashback to Jake as a young man planning to leave Canada. After a further flashback to the Horseman's activities in Montreal and his sudden departure, the novel reverts' to Jake's experiences just before he leaves for England. Part 3 oscillates between the immediate past in London and Jake's earlier experiences on his arrival there. The final part tells about the trial and its resolution and includes further flashbacks to the immediate past.

Such a complex pattern of accumulative flashbacks could perhaps confuse the reader. To safeguard against this, Richler uses dates frequently and constantly introduces significant incidents as temporal signposts in the opening paragraphs of most chapters and parts: "With his bleeding colonial heart, charged as he was with war guilt, Jake, when he had first come to London twelve years ago . . .";[1] "Yesterday, the case against him had looked shaky, very shaky, but today, Friday . . ." (62); "1951 it was and Jake . . . had been studying at McGill for three years . . ." (95); "Ben came easily, born squealing and in haste, early the following morning. May 10, 1967" (373); "More than three months passed before Jake actually stood with Harry in the dock of Number One Court of the Old Bailey . . ." (427). With these frequent references, noticeable but not obtrusive, Richler skillfully manipulates the time sequence and facilitates the reader's grasp of the chronology of events.

What does Richler achieve by employing this complex structure? In the first instance, he succeeds in imparting a tight form to this biographical study which would have been difficult to achieve with a linear organization. Though the novel remains characteristically episodic, it has a cohesion and density not evident in the preceding novels and, by beginning and ending with the trial, it acquires a structural symmetry which is emphasized by the repetition at the conclusion of the novel of certain phrases and scenes found in the opening chapters, such as the excerpts from "The Good Britons" and from Babel's *Sunset,* and the account of Jake's dream of the Horseman attacking Mengele in Paraguay. The structure also makes it possible for the reader to see how much an individual's present is haunted by his past—a theme given more extended consideration in *Joshua Then and Now*— and mirrors the protagonist's confessional, recapitulating frame of mind, which in turn constitutes a major unifying factor of the various episodes. And the structure accommodates itself readily to the traditional narrative requirement to which Richler firmly adheres: holding the reader's interest. Within the first few pages which relate events of the present, for instance, Richler whips up the reader's curiosity about why Jake's mother has come to visit him, why Nancy has ripped out a newspaper story, why Jake who is no equestrian himself has a saddle and a riding crop hidden in his cupboard, and what is the nature of his sordid crime for which he must stand trial at the Old Bailey.

St. Urbain's Horseman: Point of View and Tone

The major portion of the novel is narrated through the consciousness of Jake Hersh, whose pronounced ambivalent vision of society dictates the predominant tone. Jake, like Noah of *Son of a Smaller Hero* and Norman of *A Choice of Enemies,* is prone to disparage the conduct of those around him, but he tends to reprimand himself for this, or to wonder what prompts him to make such adverse judgments, or to question whether he is right or wrong. Richler obviously is not using Jake simply as a satiric persona to censure society; he is concerned more with analyzing Jake's conflicts and doubts. Richler apparently relegated his satirical comments on contemporary London to *Cocksure,* the novel he wrote concurrently with *St. Urbain's Horseman.*[2] He has pointed out the tonal difference between these two novels. Asked about the omission in *St. Urbain's Horseman* of an early periodical version of scenes which suggest the infidelity of the protagonist's wife, Richler replied: "Well, that particular episode in the end seemed to me to belong more to a satirical novel than this novel, and as funny as it may have been, it just didn't seem right. It seemed too too exaggerated for this kind of novel, so I just sort of cut that. . . . Yes, it seemed too far out—not for *Cocksure,* but for this."[3]

One of the clearest instances of Jake's ambivalence is his response to his wife's pleasure in gardening when they move to their new home in Hampstead. Jake, ignorant of gardening but trying to be helpful, uproots what he thinks are barren roots but which, Nancy points out to him, are peony tubers and rose bushes. Resenting her superior knowledge, he fumes to himself: "Bloody *shiksa* . . . Ontario hick, you don't know the Holy One's Secret Name, the sayings of Rabbi Akiba, or how to exorcise a dybbuk, but you would know that sort of crap . . ." (283). And observing Nancy strolling contentedly through the garden with Tom, their gardener, he sulkily describes them as "two bores out of a Thomas Hardy novel, delighting in rustic trivia, exchanging their Gentile secrets, the text derived from the Protocols of the Elders of the Compost Heap" (284). But almost simultaneously he is appalled that he could think in such terms of Nancy whom he passionately and devotedly loves and cherishes, and self-effacingly admits: "Nancy, poised and knowledgeable, the beautiful countrywoman, fallen into the hairy Jew's grasp, he truly revered and constantly deferred to" (284). Attempting to analyze his confused feelings, he considers whether he resents Nancy because of her privileged upbringing, or because gardening is alien to him, "raised on urban backyards, wherein you dumped punctured tires and watermelon husks and cracked sinks and rotting mattresses" (283), or because he feels excluded from and betrayed by Nancy's joy in gardening which she shares with their Scottish gardener. That Jake simultaneously could think so disparagingly of the woman he loves and in no way wants to mock, and then question and reprimand himself for his abuse prepares the reader to see that his pejorative remarks against others are but groping attempts to comprehend his inner inconsistency and discordance.

Richler draws heavily from his own experiences for *St. Urbain's Horseman* and has observed that Jake is closer to him than any of his other protagonists. There are several evident parallels between their lives: both, for instance, spent their boyhood and adolescence in Montreal, and escaped their stifling Jewish and Canadian environment by fleeing to London where they tried to make a name for themselves; both made trips to Israel and Germany; both are married to gentiles, have parents who are divorced, and returned in 1967 to

Montreal for their fathers' funerals. A few accounts of Jake's experiences in the novel are in fact almost verbatim reproductions from published bits of Richler's memoirs with the first person pronoun changed to "Jake." "London Province," an essay Richler wrote for the *Encounter* series of personal reminiscences of the 1940s and 1950s, provides several instances of this. Jake's faked homosexuality to embarrass a relative, his initial reaction to London, and his frustration with a silly waitress when ordering a sandwich, all have their origin in Richler's own experiences as recorded in this piece of memoir.[4] For Jake's trip to Munich, Richler draws on his own visit to Germany in 1963, an account of which appears in "The Holocaust and After."[5] And he turns to his article, "This Year in Jerusalem,"[6] an account of his visit to Israel in 1962, for some of Jake's experiences there while searching for the Horseman and for film locations.

Further similarities between Jake's and Richler's beliefs and sensibilities can be found: both share an apprehension of middle age and physical decay; both feel they belong to a frivolous generation; both are socialists but distrust the masses and professional liberals; both temper their initial harsh responses to Canadian culture; both take their art seriously, are devoted family men, and celebrate, if not live by consistently, "decency, tolerance, honor" (308). Richler makes no conscious effort to fictionalize Jake completely. Despite this, however, *St. Urbain's Horseman* is a novel, not an autobiography. It has more incidents imaginatively conceived than drawn unchanged from Richler's own experience. Most important, it maintains the double presence of author and protagonist, though it is more difficult to distinguish between the author and the mature Jake who comes to some understanding of himself after reviewing his life, than between the author and young Jake who obsessively seeks fame and feels that he has not lived life fully.

St. Urbain's Horseman: Satiric Digressions

Though Richler intends *St. Urbain's Horseman* as a sympathetic study of his troubled protagonist and relegates satire on his society to *Cocksure,* the novel is not altogether free of satirical strictures. These, however, appear in what by now can be regarded unhesitatingly as the inevitable Richlerian set scene. There are four such scenes here, which, though not wholly digressive, are certainly not organically part of the novel: the film parody of Nazi heroism; the mocking characterization of Ormsby-Fletcher; the ridiculous softball game on Hampstead Heath; and the ludicrous portrait of a Canadian Immigration Officer who encourages migration to Canada. Significantly, the last three pieces were published as separate articles.[7]

The film script, *The Good Britons*, on which Luke and Jake collaborated, is tenuously linked to the main plot since the crown prosecutor presents it as evidence of Jake's perverted taste during the trial. It also could be related to Richler's perceptive analysis of Jake's ambivalent attitude toward Germans, though its relentless satiric tone sets it apart. The excerpt from the film script which Richler presents early in the novel satirizes the contemporary tendency to glorify and exculpate German officers in modern movies. The satiric techniques Richler employs are those of straightforward parody, ironical inversion, and grotesque exaggeration. The script, presupposing that the Germans were victorious in World War II, depicts British soldiers as handsome Aryans who "fight like lions but . . . are led by donkeys" (7). The British leaders are depicted as perverted, decadent, and dominated by Jews. Field Marshall Montgomery has regressed to infancy and is beaten for his cowardice by a sadistic, half-naked Jewish WREN who is flanked by MI5 thugs all bearded and wearing skull caps. This is not one of the better instances of Richler's satirical talent, for besides the much-too-obvious inversion technique, the script, appearing in the early pages of the novel, is initially puzzling since the thematic context in which it functions has not yet been clearly established.

As Jake's defense counsel, the British solicitor, Ormsby-Fletcher, is peripherally involved in the main narrative, but Richler makes no attempt to present him as a living, individual character, choosing to use him and his wife primarily to satirize aspects of English middle-class life. Perhaps this approach was prompted by the author's realization, once again, of his inability to penetrate to the essence of the non-Jewish character, and by his awareness that he "could never know England well enough to write about it from the inside."[8] His satirical targets in his portrait of the Ormsby-Fletchers are mainly social foibles: the stiff social routine, the inflexible conversation, and the lack of spontaneity. In describing their education and social position, he parodies the Social Register, a technique used briefly in *The Acrobats* against the American dignitary at the fiesta. In the account of the Ormsby-Fletcher dinner party Richler pokes fun at Mrs. Ormsby-Fletcher's hypersensitive social conscience, echoing his treatment of Joyce in *Cocksure*. Jake features prominently toward the end of this episode. In relating Jake's coprophiliac misadventures in Ormsby-Fletcher's bathroom, Richler allows the impish writer of farce to take over from the satirist, and this farcical tone serves to isolate further this set piece from the rest of the novel.

The Hampstead Heath baseball game, like other crowd scenes from the early novels (such as the screening of Bernie's bar mitzvah in *The Apprenticeship of Duddy Kravitz* and the conduct of the inquisitive crowd during the search for Wolf's body in *Son of a Smaller Hero*), allows much scope for Richler's satirical talent. This is one of Richler's finer comic pieces. His satire is directed against the North American movie makers who have ascribed to themselves imperialistic powers in London. Describing their arrival at the park in Maseratis and Aston-Martins, Richler draws an ironic parallel with "the Raj of another dynasty" who "used to meet on the cricket pitch at Malabar" (239). The full force of his satire is directed against the craftiness and subterfuge that underline the relationships of these show-business operatives. During the baseball game arranged for pleasure and relaxation the players incongruously are not motivated by fun and spontaneity; business intrigues make them anxious and calculating. Manny, for instance, knows that it would be to his advantage if he struck out against Lou Caplan, for Lou "was ready to go with a three-picture deal with Twentieth and Manny had not been asked to direct a big budget film since *Chase*" (240); and Alfie Roberts does not expect soft pitches from Lou because he once rejected one of Lou's properties. These characters are certainly akin to those of Winkleman's coterie in *A Choice of Enemies*. The account of the earlier figures, however, is less severe, for Winkleman and his colleagues, who have significant roles in the main narrative, are presented through the tempering consciousness of the ambivalent protagonist.

The fourth satirical set piece, the account of a Canadian citizenship officer persuading the British to migrate to Canada, is briefer than the others. Richler satirizes the slickness, offhandedness, and impersonality of the citizenship officer in answering questions of potential migrants. Though the scene remains a digressive satirical interlude, it is possible to see its inclusion in the novel as a further illustration of the loneliness of Ruthy who attends the talk by the citizenship officer. Yet another of Richler's characters for whom each day is a burden, her hope of escaping her drab, empty life is frustrated by the cold, insensitive officer.

In addition to these entertaining but digressive pieces, there are other passages which, though not exactly set scenes, have only a slight narrative and thematic significance. One such passage relates Jake's adventures in London with Herky, his brother-in-law. Herky is professionally interested in washrooms and wants to spend his holiday in London touring the public facilities. Richler's portrait of him verges on caricature, and the account of his activities in London, particularly his arrest in Harrod's for taking photographs of the toilet facilities, is evidently intended as a comic byplay. Richler, however, makes some use of the Harrod incident for suspense when early in the novel he makes Jake tell Nancy that the happenings in Harrod's toilets, which are left unspecified, cannot be used against him since it "never made the charge sheet" (37).

Another passage that is not really digested within the novel is the extended narration of Duddy Kravitz's investment in reducing pills during the 1950s in Montreal. Like the account of Herky in London, this is essentially a comic interlude with little bearing on the central theme and narrative other than perhaps to help establish an authenticity of place and time. Duddy also appears in the present sequence of the novel as a visitor to London. In his portrayal of this older Duddy, Richler accents the ironies in his life: now a millionaire, but aging and desirous of a warm home and an affectionate wife, he is married to a young actress, whose bustling concern with her career makes her insensitive to Duddy's needs, just as Duddy's obsessive pursuit of his land in *The Apprenticeship of Duddy Kravitz* made him oblivious to the feelings of others. Richler's inclusion of Duddy's London visit is more relevant as a postscript to the earlier novel than as an integral part of *St. Urbain's Horseman*. But perhaps its incorporation in this inclusive novel (which offers many detailed miscellaneous accounts of such things as Mensa tests, the mechanics of toilets, and the history of Canadian and Jewish criminals tried at the Old Bailey) should not too readily be construed as entirely digressive.

St. Urbain's Horseman: Ethical Sphere

In *St. Urbain's Horseman* Richler employs the most complex and challenging symbol in all his novels: the Horseman. Critics have offered various readings of this elusive figure: Robert Brandeis, for instance, sees him as Jake's "conscience and mentor"; Warren Tallman believes he is Jake's "vision of a redeeming manhood for Jewish men"; David Sheps takes him as "the messianic figure, the redemptive deliverer of his people"; Donald Cameron suggests he represents "truth and courage"; and Wilfred Cude, identifying the Horseman with the golem which he considers a metaphor for the triumph of art, states that "Jake's avoidance of the seamy side of the [historical] golem is an indication of his determination to see nothing but the heroic in his cousin Joey."[9] Each of these critics gives the Horseman a single, fixated symbolic meaning. However, it appears that Richler intends him to function as a floating symbol with multiple meanings which vary in the different spheres of the novel.

Richler considers Jake's experiences, like Mortimer's in *Cocksure*, in four contiguous spheres of human activity: the domestic, the social, the ethnical, and the professional or artistic. In the domestic and social spheres the Horseman is an ethical symbol: he is a false god in whom Jake initially puts his trust. In the ethnic sphere, he is, when linked with the motif of Jake's dreams and nightmares, part of Richler's ambitious effort to create a myth for the contemporary Jew's experience—a factor which paradoxically makes this, Richler's most all-embracing work, the most "Jewish" of his novels. In the artistic sphere the Horseman represents the artist's desire for participation which is constantly in conflict with his inherent role as an observer.

In his social and domestic life, Jake is bewildered when confronted with spiritual and ethical choices. Life proves to be "too complicated . . . too spiky" (18) for him. He craves "answers, a revelation, something out there, a certitude" (302). Initially, the Horseman provides him with the answers. He becomes the Horseman's "acolyte," and the Horseman becomes his "moral editor" (311). On one occasion, tucking Sammy, his seven-year-old son, into bed, Jake has to restrain himself from telling him that he has replaced God with the Horseman. At the end of the novel, however, as he stands with the Horseman's revolver in his hand, absently contemplating suicide, he comes to realize that he, like the biblical Aaron, has been worshipping a false god: "I want to find out who I am, he had told Issy Hersh. It's taken years, but now I know. Who am I? Well, I'm not Hedda Gabler. I'm Aaron, maybe" (465).[10] Richler points up this epiphany by quoting in full at this point the First Commandment, which warns against false gods and graven images. Jake eventually discovers for himself that his mentor is no idealist but a blackmailer, a bigamist, a liar, a gigolo, and a dope-pedlar. Prior to this discovery, Jake used to defend the Horseman against all pejorative remarks. However, the older Jake, through whose consciousness the novel is narrated, commenting on an abortive trip to New York undertaken in his youth when he was mistaken for the Horseman, admits that this incident was "the true beginning, albeit inadvertent, of what was to be his ride to ruin with St. Urbain's Horseman" (95). Nancy, who speaks with the truth of a chorus figure, also blames the Horseman for Jake's misfortunes. Even Jake's youthful, romantic view of the Horseman as a knight in shining armor is shattered when, toward the end of the novel, Jake discovers that Joey's revolver, which so intrigued him as a boy and added to Joey's romantic aura, fires only blanks.

On the ethical level it is possible to see the Horseman, who after his initial appearance in the novel becomes a shadowy figure or a presence rather than a living entity, as Jake's alter ego, or in Jungian terms, as his shadow with which he eventually comes to grips. Significantly, in an early version of the first section of the novel published in *Tamarack Review*[11] and in several drafts of the novel (among Richler's papers in the University of Calgary Library), it is Jake himself who dreams of hunting down Mengele. No mention is made of Joey, the Horseman. Jake, who self-admittedly is filled with doubts and contradictions and has done all the "right wrong things" (303), is sedentary, responsible, and stands for traditional and spiritual values. The Horseman, conversely, is adventurous, dionysian, self-centered, assertive, and amoral. Uncle Abe is acknowledging their antithetical nature when he tells Jake: "I do not compare you with him. You're a good Jewish boy" (409). Yet their oneness is suggested by their similar initials (a factor Richler had not yet introduced in a very early version of the novel, where Joey is called "Cousin Moe"),[12] by Jake's obsessive preoccupation with the Horseman, by the recurring incidents of mistaken identity (at the American border and at Canada House, for instance), and by the similarity between the two observed by others such as the RCAF officer who, referring to the Horseman by his alias, says: "It doesn't surprise me that this Jessie Hope bird is your cousin" (269).

Jake's questioning of the Horseman's dubious values begins to appear midway through the novel, particularly in his relationship with members of the Hersh family, both individually and collectively. The Horseman hates the Hershes whom he blames for the death of his father, Baruch, and for abandoning himself, his brother and sister, and his mother. Before he comes to realize that he has been worshipping a false god, Jake time and again shares this hatred even though Hanna tells him that Baruch, an irresponsible and cruel man, was not wholly blameless. However, Jake learns to tolerate and to understand the Hershes in spite of their failings for which his sometime mentor relentlessly molests them. An early indication of this is Jake's indignation when he learns from Chava, the Horseman's Israeli wife, of the Horseman's mocking remark that had the Hershes participated in the 1948 siege of Jerusalem, they would have been the first to wave the white flag.

Jake's increasing rejection of the Horseman's pejorative assessment of the Hershes becomes evident in his mixed response to them when he returns to Montreal for his father's funeral. He is much more kindly disposed to the family and feels "closer to them than he had in years" (403). Like Noah Adler of *Son of a Smaller Hero,* he feels "cradled" (396) by this world and, despite its shortcomings, he reveals a generosity of spirit to its way of life which exceeds Noah's when he returns to the Adler fold. Jake even comes to accept that his sheltered life in London as a fairly well paid director, removed from the problems of everyday living, has tended to make him annoyingly supercilious. Rifka, his sister, alerts him to this: "You come here once a year maybe and you booze from morning until night and stir up trouble. Then you fly off again. Who needs you anyway?" (403). Uncle Abe, explaining the conflicts and struggles of the Jews to be accepted in Montreal, makes a similar observation: "Listen, you don't live here. In your rarified world, film people, writers, directors, actors, it hardly matters that this one's a Jew, that one's black. . . . You lead a sheltered life, my young friend. We live here in the real world, and let me tell you it's a lot better today than it was when I was a youngster" (407). Throughout the novel Uncle Abe is a possible villain involved in betraying Joey, and his comments are not to be accepted unquestioningly. His sentiments here, however, would appear to have authorial sanction, for they are similar to Richler's observation about himself: he has stated in an interview that he does not want to continue living "in such a sheltered society as I have."[13]

Uncle Abe is Richler's mouthpiece on another occasion when he speaks against the hollow, trendy militancy of the young, which Richler himself excoriates in his essay, "A With-It Professor Proudly Wearing a Nehru Jacket."[14] Since Abe echoes the author's sentiments at times, the reader hesitates to share Jake's distrust of him. Jake himself begins to have second thoughts about his uncle and his involvement in Joey's accident. Though the accident remains obscure, it is quite possible, as Uncle Abe and Jenny suggest, that it was in fact a jealous husband who had engineered it rather than the Quebecois whom the Horseman taunted. Early in the novel, even though Jake dislikes Uncle Abe, he has "to allow" that Uncle Abe is not "utterly without conscience" (102). And when he angrily accuses Uncle Abe and the other uncles of abandoning Baruch and Joey, he discovers that this is not wholly true—a realization which initially frustrates him since it robs him of justification for disliking his uncles: "His uncles guffawed; they retorted heatedly, but justifiably, that any (or almost any) Hersh could get work with one another of them, which only fired Jake's anger more" (172).

The evening before his departure from Montreal for London after a week spent mourning his father's death, Jake manhandles Irwin, Uncle Abe's spoilt son, stomping on his toes, elbowing him in the stomach, and slapping him across the face. And, as he walks away from the sobbing Irwin, he announces with quiet fury to an aghast Uncle Abe: "My grandfather didn't come here steerage, Baruch didn't die in penury, Joey wasn't driven out of town, so that this jelly, this nose-picker, this sports nut, this lump of shit, your son, should inherit the earth" (412). This incident, coming soon after Jake's growing acceptance of members of the Hersh family, dramatically embodies his innate ambivalence and inconsistency.

Though Jake was initially annoyed by his father's prejudicial resentment of his marriage to a gentile, he is generally tolerant of him and exhibits filial warmth. What strikes the mature Jake most forcefully about his relationship with his father are the ironical parallels of their lives. He remembers the time his father refused to give alms to a war veteran, skeptically questioning whether the man was an authentic casualty of war; and he immediately recalls "with a chill of shame" (399) his own treatment of Tom, his gardener, whose needs he himself doubts. His rude, puerile treatment of the English constable, Hoare, makes him admit ruefully to Nancy: "We're all becoming our fathers, you know . . . Luke's joined the Garrick Club and I'm turning out a fool" (288). And he remembers again with guilt that as "a St. Urbain Street boy he had, God forgive him, been ashamed of his parents' Yiddish accent. Now that he lived in Hampstead, Sammy (and soon Molly and Ben too, he supposed) mocked his immigrant's twang" (6)—which, incidentally, is another parallel between Jake and Richler, who makes a similar comment about his family life in England: ". . . I was ashamed of my parents' Yiddish accent as a kid. Now my kids are ashamed of my Canadian immigrant's accent."[15]

Jake is also struck by the irony in the life of the Horseman's sister, Jenny, whom the Horseman never liked. Independent, vibrant, and resourceful, but poor, she realizes that her only way out of the ghetto is through learning. Sadly, however, her interest in literature, her favorite subject, is that of the dilettante and the social climber. When she finally becomes a member of the sophisticated circle of Toronto, she perceives with telling irony that it is the unsophisticated but natural Hanna in whom her cultured friends are interested. Her rebellion against the Hershes can be contrasted with Noah's in *Son of a Smaller Hero,* for while Noah leaves the fold inspired by a search for ideals and truths, Jenny is prompted by a sense of spite. Her rebellion, like Ruthy Bone's in *The Incomparable Atuk,* is intended as a slap to the family, and it means something only if it hurts and embarrasses the Hershes. Unlike Ruthy Bone, however, Jenny is not farcically dismissed. The pathos of her self-estrangement from the Hershes is emphasized: she is not missed by them, a fact which Jake, kinder to her than her brother, the Horseman, refrains from telling her.

Hanna, the Horseman's mother, is portrayed as an engaging, Dickensian eccentric. Her characterization is quite vibrant, even though she appears in just a few scenes. Her earthiness and honesty are in direct contrast to the superficiality and trendiness of the sophisticated world which Jenny inhabits. A blindly devoted, self-sacrificial mother, she is treated by the Horseman with unbecoming indifference. Jake, on the other hand, is very much devoted to her, and many of his achievements are more gratifying to him because they win her approval. His relationship with her is the only one that reflects no conflicting, ambivalent feelings on his part.

His own mother, however, evokes strong ambivalence in him. She appears to be an aging version of Noah's. The Hershes whom Jake tries to tolerate have all featured in his past experience or are safely distanced in Montreal. However, his mother, who still disapproves of his mixed marriage, appears in the current time sequence of the novel, and is palpably present in Jake's London home during his trial. Her immediate presence makes it difficult for him to objectify and to analyze his feelings toward her. What Richler depicts is his spontaneous resentment toward an interfering mother rather than feelings recollected and vacillatingly examined, which on the whole informs his response to the other Hershes. The scenes in which she appears

constitute a brief study of the trying relationship between an exasper-
ated son and a clinging mother, but they also serve dramatically to
heighten the tension in Jake's home during his trial. At the end of
the novel, after his mother has returned to Montreal, Jake objectively
though briefly contemplates his relationship with her and exhibits
characteristically mixed feelings: "He wept for his mother, who de-
served a more loving son" (464). This significantly is much more
than Jake's mentor offers his own mother.

Before he discerns the Horseman to be a false god, Jake cultivates
his mindless hatred of the persecutors of Jews, particularly of the
Germans, all of whom he indiscriminately considers to be Nazis.
Many of Richler's early protagonists reveal in one way or another an
ambivalent response to Germans. In *Son of a Smaller Hero* Noah is
conscious of the Nazis' brutal treatment of the Jews, but rejects the
atavistic hatred which a Polish Jew, a survivor of the extermination
camps, seeks to instill in the Jewish youths of the Montreal ghetto.
In *The Acrobats* and *A Choice of Enemies* André and Norman display
both resentment of and generosity to their German rivals.

Richler himself has a mixed response: he satirizes Cohen's use of
the Nazi persecution of the Jews to justify his own exploitation of the
less fortunate in *The Apprenticeship of Duddy Kravitz,* yet in *Cocksure* he
rejects the facile liberal attitude of Lord Woodcock who seeks to forgive and forget the Nazi atrocities. Richler, as his impassioned essay
"The Holocaust and After" reveals, is deeply disturbed by the savage
genocide of the Jews and exhibits a sweeping hatred of Germans:
"The Germans are still an abomination to me. I do not mourn for
Cologne, albeit decimated for no useful military purpose. I rejoice in
the crash of each German Starfighter. No public event in recent years
has thrilled me more than the hunting down of Adolf Eichmann. I
am not touched by the Berlin Wall."[16] Despite the anger here, the
essay makes clear that what really annoys Richler is contemporary society's attempt to gloss over this moral blotch on human history. In
the interest of morality and justice, Richler states, the atrocities committed against the Jews should never be allowed to be forgotten. In
an interview with Donald Cameron he emphasizes this point when
accounting for his hatred of Germans:

Cameron: Does your hatred of the Germans have to do with your moral-
          ism? Are you saying, Look there's a horror here?
Richler: Yes. We've lived through two great horrors, in our time, the

murder of the Jews and Hiroshima, and the rest disappears. This is what we lived through in our time and one must, you know, figure out where he stands in relation to it . . .[17]

Jake exhibits a similar ambivalence to Germans. Initially, like the Horseman, he hates them mindlessly. In his trial, when asked by the crown prosecutor whether he personally finds Germans abhorrent, he evades the question, pretending to be appalled: "Why . . . that would make me a racist, sir" (70). But immediately after, he envisions, as he does in the first sentence of the novel, the Horseman stalking Dr. Mengele to wreak vengeance on him for his brutal treatment of the Jews. And when Nancy asks how so many years after the war he can still hate Germans, he tells her he could do so easily "unto the tenth generation" (71). His hatred is stoked by his deeply ingrained terror of the Nazis which induces nightmares of "extermination officers" (73) slaughtering his three children, by the documents and photographs of Nazi atrocities collected by himself and the Horseman, and by the liturgical solemnity of a witness's response at the war trials at Frankfurt which continually rings in his ears:

"Mengele cannot have been there all the time."
"In my opinion always. Night and day." (271)

In Germany, where his obsessive quest for the Horseman takes him, the irrationality of Jake's hatred is shown in his drunken abuse of the officers of the Canadian Armed Forces base in Germany. One officer significantly implies that Jake's abusive comments on Germans are no different from the Horseman's.

That Jake is incapable of the Horseman's malignant hatred, however, is dramatically revealed in the scene where he bumps into a German woman on a Munich street and quickly apologizes, "instead of following through with his shoulder and stamping on her. Hatred was a discipline. He would have to train harder, that's all" (262). Though he tries to adopt the Horseman's attitude and suppress his accommodating nature, Jake nevertheless gradually perceives that Joey's hatred lacks any moral basis which would provide some justification for his vengeance. Like the ambiguous golem, the Horseman is a "body without a soul" (270). He is, as a Jewish army chaplain tells Jake, "without an interest in metaphysics" (265). He hunts down Nazis and fights for the Israeli cause without believing in God or in the Jewish tradition and religion, seeking only to satisfy his craving for vengeance which makes him cruel and exploitative. He once shot in cold blood a surrendering Jewish rabbi during the Arab siege of Jerusalem in 1948. His treatment of Chava, his Israeli wife, and of Ruthy, his Anglo-Jewish fiancée, bewilders his acolyte, who significantly feels it is his duty to make redress. The Horseman's behavior does not wholly contradict Uncle Abe's assumption that he probably died while operating a smuggling ring in South America rather than while heroically attempting to track down Mengele.

The Horseman's lack of social conscience revealed in his attitude toward his own family and community and toward individuals like Chava and Ruthy sets him apart from Jake, who is constantly bothered by the inconsistency between his privileged status and his socialist beliefs. Jake feels guilty when he sets his good fortune against the lot of the suffering masses. Of his first movie, dismissed by him as another "interesting film for the circuit," he says: "The energy he and others had expended, the one million two hundred thousand dollars they had consumed, could have been used much more beneficially providing shelter for the homeless, food for the hungry. So much for honour, so much for grace" (292). Yet his actions belie his socialist sentiments. He is absorbed neurotically in preparing to defend his family against the anticipated attack of the starving hordes rather than in helping them. And although he initially hopes to further his son's sense of social justice by employing Tom, the gardener, he fires him, depriving him of desperately needed wages because "he was made to feel an intruder in his own garden" (285). Jake is aware that he does not put his socialist sentiments into practice: "I, Jacob Hersh . . . paid £15,000 *not* to direct a fun film, made love to my wife on crisp clean sheets, sent my progeny to private schools, worried about corpulence gained through overindulgence and play hours lost through overimbibing. . . . While the rich got richer and the poor poorer, I survived nicely" (89–90). And he understands why Elijah, whom the Jews believe to be a special protector of the sick, the poor, and the harassed, never comes "to sip from his silver wine cup at the Passover table" (89).

A dramatic illustration of Jake's inconsistent socialism is the extended account of his involvement with the perverted malcontent, Harry Stein. Like Duddy Kravitz, though much less blameless and more deliberately vindictive, Harry is perceived as a victim of environment and circumstances. Born in a London slum and a waif during the war, Harry was trained by his impoverished father, an embittered man himself, to hate the rich. Jake compares his own adolescent romanticized vision of the London blitz with the harsh actuality of Harry's experience:

> Oh to be blitzed, Jake used to dream, orphaned and adopted by M-G-M; but it was something else for prickly Harry Stein. Even before the *Luftwaffe* struck, ten-year-old Harry, scruffy and sty-ridden, was uprooted from his Stepney council school, tagged, issued a gas mask, and shoveled into a train crammed with squealing mums and babes, other slum kids (some covered with septic sores, still more lice-infested), and frantic teachers; a train without food and insufficient toilets, each one at flood-tide, the floor slithery; to be finally disgorged on a station platform in the outer wilds of Buckinghamshire, where the ill-tempered gentry, aghast to discover such urban pestilence in their midst, had nevertheless foregathered to take their pick. (21–22)

Jake's laughter at his own idealized conception of the war and his recounting of Harry's childhood convey his underlying sympathy for Harry though he is aware of his prickliness and ill will. Harry invites Jake to consider the injustice of his present situation: adjudged by Mensa to be among the top two percent in I.Q., Harry works for a pittance in a "tiny cell where he consumed his days" (220) at a job which ironically brings him into servile contact with the despised rich. Despite his restrained sympathy for Stein, however, Jake is wary of him, knowing that he is a reprehensible man, capable of blackmail, of maliciously scratching parked Rolls-Royces, and of making atrociously obscene telephone calls.

Besides dramatically illustrating Jake's troubled social conscience, Harry Stein plays a significant role in the main narrative, that is, Jake's indictment for rape. He has yet another function: like the Horseman, he serves as Jake's alter ego. Several incidents and comments underline this. Nancy, for instance, observes that "Harry fascinates" (57) Jake, who himself significantly often addresses Harry by the hypocoristic "Hershel," a form of his own surname. Jake expresses a "sneaking admiration" (340) for some of Harry's vindictive acts, which would support Harry's assertion to Jake that "I've got the courage to do things you only dream of" (374). At times Jake's Steinian qualities do come to the surface, as in his vengefully spraying his crotchety neighbor's rhododendrons with lime, in his vindictively leading a Canadian Forces officer in Germany to believe that a CBC film unit intends to make a feature on lesbianism in the Armed Forces, and in his irrationally resenting Nancy's privileged upbringing. In Jake's relationship with his family and with his society, then, the Horseman is a symbol of false values. At the end of the novel Jake wonders whether the Horseman "was a distorting mirror and we each took the self-justifying image we required of him?" (464). Richler himself affirms this function when asked to explain the Horseman's role in the novel:

It depends who's looking at what, what happened, and we bring our own needs. So you could say, he's whatever you need, that's as far as I can go. If you look back at it all—Jenny said he was in love with her and wanted to screw her, Abe had—everyone brings their own problems to him. So it's a kind of distorting mirror figure, really.[18]

Besides Jake, five characters are linked to the Horseman when he functions as a symbol of dubious ethics. Jenny, absorbed by sensuality, believes that Joey returned to Montreal for incestuous reasons; Uncle Abe, to justify his own chicanery, sees him as a blackmailer, a gigolo, a gambler, and a liar; Hanna, yearning for lost motherhood, continues to consider him as the frail child she gave birth to in a miner's shanty in the Northwest Territories; Chava, believing him to be the son of a rich family, clutches onto him as her passport from the hard life in the kibbutz; and Ruthy, filled with social aspirations, wants to marry into the Old French Jewish family de la Hersh, to which the Horseman led her to believe he belongs.

St. Urbain's Horseman: The Ethnic Sphere

His generation of Jews, Richler observes, having "not gone like sheep to the slaughterhouse" in Dachau and Auschwitz and being "too fastidious to punish Arab villlages with napalm," did not "fit a mythology" (308). By employing the figure of the Horseman and the cyclical progression from dreams to nightmares of horsemanship, Richler attempts to create a myth that would give expression to their common predicament.

Jake shares in his people's collective memory of persecutions and injustices which scream for a defender and avenger. Initially, he believes in the possibility of the Jews becoming assertive and heroic, shedding their image as a people who accept unprotestingly persecution and exploitation as their lot. The Horseman is the symbol of this aspiration. He avenges the wrongs against the Jews in Montreal, in Israel, and in Germany, and his current task in the novel is hunting down the arch-enemy of the Jews, Dr. Mengele, "the butcher of Auschwitz." For Jake, the Horseman astride his magnificent Pleven stallion, "galloping, thundering. Planning fresh campaigns, more daring manoeuvres" (35), is the perfect image of dignity and courage. His endeavors mean that the Jews will no longer be vulnerable, no longer be given to groveling compliance like Uncle Abe when faced with anti-Semitism in Quebec, and no longer be subjected to the indignity of accepting German reparation, for which the Horseman forbids Chava to apply. Jake continuously dreams of the endeavors of the Horseman, portrayed as the "Jewish Batman" and as the golem of whom Jake says: he "was made out of clay by Rabbi Judah Ben Bezalel in the sixteenth century to defend the Jews of Prague from a pogrom and, to my mind, still wanders the world turning up wherever a defender is most needed" (270).

In Jake's journal, where he records various details and facts about the Horseman, there are four references to horses in relation to Jews that underline their aspiration to become horsemen. The first reference is an extract from Isaac Babel's play, *Sunset* (or more precisely from Richler's adaptation of this play).[19] The Jewish cavalryman, Levka, tells the old marriage-broker, Arye-Leib, that "when a Jew gets on a horse he stops being a Jew . . ." (34). Levka does not mean that he ethnically ceases to be a Jew but that he is no longer an undignified figure of easy exploitation. In Richler's dramatization Levka is an assertive soldier bedecked in the hussar's full-dress uniform, a golden forage cap, a long, full cloak, and carries a curved sabre. The second reference is to Monroe Stahr's observation from *The Last Tycoon* that the Jews have taken over the worship of horses. In F. Scott Fitzgerald's novel Monroe Stahr is a Hollywood producer. Listening to the enthusiasm with which certain of his Jewish colleagues were talking of a very fast horse, he "guessed that the Jews had taken over the worship of horses as a symbol—for years it had been the Cossacks mounted and the Jews on foot. Now the Jews had horses, and it gave them a sense of extraordinary well-being and power."[20] The third reference is simply the title of Alberto Gerchunoff's *The Jewish Gauchos of the Pampas (Los Gauchos Judios)*,[21] a work in which the Jewish immigrants to Argentina are shown to have become resourceful and dig-

nified cowboys. And the fourth is apparently a brief jotting on the
mounted courier system of the Rothschilds—"The web of messen-
gers" (34)—which before the introduction of the telegraph was more
efficient than the government couriers.

The section of the journal where these references are found, Jake
observes early in the novel, is "still sadly incomplete" (33). It remains incomplete at the end, for the crusading Horseman, the symbol of Jewish emergent assertiveness, is killed in an aircrash while
tracking Mengele in South America. Jake, the Horseman's advocate,
believes that he was killed by Mengele. However, he does not dis-
count the possibility that the Jewish community in South America,
fearful of provoking reprisal from Mengele's followers should the
Horseman kidnap Mengele, could have caused the Horseman's death.
Jake's suspicion of Jewish complicity counters Uncle Abe's conviction
that the Horseman died while engaged in a smuggling operation.
The reader becomes aware that the comments relevant to the Horseman as a symbol of the Jewish ancestral memory are always given
through Jake's dreams, his mind's eye, or his conjectures. The comments of others, like Uncle Abe, are relevant to the Horseman's function as a false god in the ethical sphere of the novel.

In Richler's account of incidents after Jake learns of the death of
Joey, three important contiguous points should be noted. First, Jake
states that he will now become St. Urbain's avenging Horseman and,
having dreamed of himself taking revenge on Mengele, changes the
entry of the Horseman's death in his journal to "presumed dead"
(467). Second, the novel ends with a passage that is virtually similar
to the opening paragraphs. Third, the very significant change between these two passages (other than Jake himself becoming the
Horseman) is that the "dream" of the first page has become a "nightmare"—the word is mentioned twice—in the final passage. By suggesting that the Horseman is presumed dead and that Jake aspires
toward becoming the Horseman, Richler is underlining the fact that
the aspiration of becoming a horseman is an ingrained aspect of the
Jewish collective unconscious. In ending the novel where it begins,
Richler shows that though this hope is unconquerable, it is a futile
aspiration. Jake can resolve to become and can dream of becoming
the Horseman, but like the Horseman he will fail.

That Jake's dream of the Horseman ultimately becomes a nightmare symbolically reflects this futility. In his essay, "Master of
Dreams,"[22] Leslie Fiedler describes Joseph's dreaming of power in

Genesis, as part of a single grand mythic plot which, in various manifestations, is presumed to underlie all Jewish literature and cultural activities. Joseph dreams of the whole world bowing down to him as a viceroy of the mightiest king on earth, and does realize his dream. What Fiedler ignores, however, is the eventual transformation of the dream into a nightmare as the Egyptians enslave Joseph's descendants. In "Jewish Dreams and Nightmares," Robert Alter's response to Fiedler's essay, the nightmare is suggested as the more appropriate symbol of the Jewish experience. Referring to Kafka's nightmarish world, Alter shows that the Jew is an oppressed not a viceregal figure. He quotes a relevant passage from Kafka's tale, "An Old Manuscript," which tells of a conquered people's inability to deal with their implacable nomadic oppressors:

> From my stock, too, they have taken many good articles. But I cannot complain when I see how the butcher, for instance, suffers across the street. As soon as he brings in any meat the nomads snatch it all from him and gobble it up. Even their horses devour flesh; often enough a horseman and his horses are lying side by side, both of them gnawing at the same joint, one on either end. The butcher is nervous and does not dare to stop his deliveries of meat. We understand that, however, and subscribe money to keep him going. If the nomads got no meat, who knows what they might think of doing.

Commenting on the passage, Alter says, "One can see a distinctly familiar response of the Jews to violence and impending disaster—the attempt to buy off calamity, to temporize with it."[23]

Richler's vision of the contemporary Jew incorporates both the dream and the nightmare. Joey the Horseman, like his biblical namesake, aspires toward dignity and power; and Jake, like the biblical Jacob, shares in his aspiration. Their dream, however, is an impossible dream of the unattainable, for either because of their omnipresent enemies or their own passive, temporizing people (which Jake conjectures caused the death of the Horseman in South America), the ever-resurging dream cyclically becomes a nightmare. Several other incidents illustrate this mythic conception of the Jewish dream and nightmare of horsemanship. Joey, Jake believes, is routed and exiled from Montreal because he sought to avenge the Jews. Uncle Abe tells Jake that the Jews cannot afford the Horseman's approach for that would lead to their destruction; it is better to temporize with and buy off calamity. Joey's avenging trip to South America, Uncle Abe

says, is no different from his acts of vengeance in Montreal: "it makes
trouble for the Jews in Asunción, that's all" (411). The way for Israel
to survive is also through compromising, through accepting German
reparation, and through flagrant promotion of tourism and commercial opportunism.

Jake's horsemanly treatment of the German *au pair* girl is an instance of the dream becoming a nightmare. Jake sees Ingrid Loebner's
father as a potential Mengele. He was a dentist who "must have been
busy during the war, extracting gold fillings from Jews" (433). Ingrid's patronizing comment that Jake is likable even though he is a
Jew angers him. He roughly throws her out of his house—a pale im-
itation of Joey's planned vengeance on Mengele, but nevertheless a
horsemanly act, which, as Harry points out, leads into the nightmare
of the trial: "If you hadn't heaved her out of the house, she never
would have gone to the cops" (421). During the trial Jake finds he
too has to temporize with and buy off calamity.

St. Urbain's Horseman: The Artistic Sphere

In addition to his mythopoeic significance and his function as a
symbol of false values, the Horseman in his relationship with Jake
represents the personal conflict of some creative artists between their
desire for participation and their occupational role of observers. The
young Jake sees the Horseman as a romantic, adventurous Hemingway hero who has been a commercial pilot, a professional football
player, had ridden with Randolph Scott, and was once married to a
Hollywood starlet. He appears to be Duddy's fictitious brother, Bradley, come to life. On Joey's return to Montreal in a sleek sports car
Jake describes him in heroic terms: "the MG could have been a magnificent stallion and Cousin Joey a knight returned from a foreign
crusade" (129). His admiration grows when he discovers that the
RCMP is investigating Joey and that McCarthy has blacklisted him.

Jake's regard for the Horseman's mode of living continues unabated into adulthood. Even when he achieves some recognition as a
film director, he considers his work to be meaningless when compared to the Horseman's active participation in causes such as the
Spanish liberation, the establishment of Israel, and meting out vengeance on Nazi war criminals. Sitting passively in what Jake wishfully
calls his "attic aerie" (33), he often daydreams of the Horseman:
". . . maybe this very minute, he is out riding somewhere. Over the

olive-green hills of the Upper Galilee or maybe in Mexico again. Or Catalonia. But, most likely, in Paraguay" (34). When Jake envisions the Horseman on heroic missions, he tends to linger over romantic place names and images, as the previous passage and this one indicate: "Neighing, the stallion rears, obliging the Horseman to dig his stirrups in. Eventually he slows. Still in the highlands, emerging from the dense forest to scan the scrub below, he strains to find the unmarked road that winds into the jungle, between Puerto San Vincente and the border fortress of Carlos Antonio López" (175). The more Jake contemplates the heroic, dionysian Horseman, the less is his pleasure in sedentary pursuits and in literature, which now "fills him with ennui."

Literature, once his consolation, was no longer enough. To read of meanness in others, promiscuity well observed or greed understood, to discover his own inadequacies shared no longer licensed them, any more than all the deaths that had come before could begin to make his own endurable.
Oh Horseman, Horseman, where are you? (302)

Like Norman of *A Choice of Enemies,* Jake blames his quandary partly on his untimely generation. Eleven years younger than the Horseman, he was born too late for involvement in the Spanish Civil War, World War II, Hiroshima, the Israeli War of Independence, McCarthyism, and Korea. Conversely, he was born too early for involvement with Vietnam and the revolutionary activities of the young radicals of the 1960s. His generation is doomed to be "ever observers, never participants" (87). Richler does not resolve this artistic conflict in the novel. (In general, the symbolic function of the Horseman in this sphere is peripheral when compared to his other functions.) Of some significance, however, is that, at the end of the novel, when the Horseman is presumed dead, Jake, encouraged by his wife and Luke, finally decides to return to his creative endeavors.

Emulating his adventurous cousin, Jake as a young man seeks his fortune outside Canada. He makes an attempt to migrate to New York but is thwarted by American immigration officers who mistake him for the blacklisted Horseman. Eventually he escapes to London, convinced that he cannot realize his ambitions in a culturally barren environment peopled by second-rate artists at whom, like Richler's earlier protagonists, he scoffs. The mature Jake stands apart from the young Jake who emulates the Horseman's tendency to blame others for his problems, and though he continues to make adverse comments on Canada, he re-examines his motives for criticizing his homeland and finds himself wanting: "Fulminating in Montreal, he could agree with Auden that the dominions were *tiefste Provinz*. Scornful of all things home-baked, he was at one with Dr. Johnson, finding his country a cold and uninviting region. As his father had blamed the *goyim* for all his inadequacies . . . so Jake had foolishly held Canada culpable for all his discontents" (301–2). Such honest self-scrutiny characterizes Jake who, at thirty-seven, is obviously experiencing a climacteric. But as is indicated yet again by his unabated adverse comments on Canada in spite of his self-awareness, Jake is a man caught up by inconsistency and ambivalence.

In his early novels Richler occasionally and restrictively employs symbols and allegories, such as the burning of the giant falla in *The Acrobats*, the *horah* which Noah wants both to join and to leave in *Son of a Smaller Hero*, Norman's balloon in *A Choice of Enemies*, and the Old One's disapproval of Atuk's mixed marriage in *The Incomparable Atuk*. But in none of these novels are these techniques used so organically and extensively as in *St. Urbain's Horseman*. The multiple co-existing symbolic and allegorical functions of the Horseman, together with the involved narrative, the skillful structural use of flashbacks, the extensive gallery of memorable minor characters, and the penetrating study of the ambivalent protagonist, make *St. Urbain's Horseman* a very richly textured work and have encouraged several critics to consider this Richler's best novel.

Joshua Then and Now

Nine years after *St. Urbain's Horseman* Richler published *Joshua Then and Now*, his eighth novel, which could be read as a companion piece or a sequel to the earlier work. The protagonist, Joshua Shapiro, is similar in temperament and sensibility to Jake Hersh. Richler could be speaking of Jake when he describes Joshua as a man "charged with contradictions" who "sent his children to private schools and complained in other people's houses about being the father of children who attended private schools."[24] Though Joshua is perhaps not as intensely introspective as Jake, he exhibits Jake's ambivalent response to his own family and people. Both are moral figures adhering to traditional spiritual values, yet they have a perceptible streak of malice in them. Both experience nightmares originating from fear of real or imagined Nazi butchers and from apprehension about their gentile wives' infidelity with someone more ethnically compatible. Both were born in Montreal and lived in similar domestic and communal environments, though particulars differ. Both developed artistic interests—Jake as a film director and Joshua as a journalist—and fled their constricting homeland for Paris, Spain, and London. Like Jake, Joshua has become obsessively conscious of his mortality. Both novels have long flashbacks to the protagonists' childhood in Montreal and later years in Europe. The current action of the earlier novel occurs in 1967 when Jake is in his late thirties; in *Joshua Then and Now* it is 1977 and Joshua is ten years older than his predecessor.

Richler's plotting of *Joshua Then and Now* derives much from *St. Urbain's Horseman*. Each novel has two fairly integrated yet separate plots, one set in the present and the other in the past. In both, the first is relatively more engrossing and complex. In *St. Urbain's Horseman* Jake is implicated in a sex scandal which leads to his trial at the Old Bailey. In this novel Joshua, recuperating from a critical car accident, is plagued by problems. His wife Pauline has disappeared from the hospital where she had been taken after her nervous breakdown, brought on by the suicide of her playboy brother, Kevin. She felt responsible for his death since she had refused to give false testimony that might have acquitted him of embezzlement. Joshua's career is jeopardized by press reports of his supposed homosexuality which started with the publication of letters he and a fellow writer, Sidney Murdoch, had mischievously concocted with the intention of selling them to unsuspecting universities keen on acquiring literary manuscripts. Joshua is concerned also that Officer McMaster knows of his breaking into the homes of Westmount colleagues to commit such malicious acts of vandalism as peeling labels off vintage wine bottles, cunningly defacing valuable paintings, and planting stolen money. All these problems are resolved in the end: McMaster does not incriminate him; his reputation as a homosexual is proved unfounded; and a recuperating Pauline returns home safely.

The account of Joshua's experiences from boyhood to the present which constitutes the other plot (or perhaps can be taken as an extension of the current narrative) is more straightforward, episodic, and uncomplicated. In *St. Urbain's Horseman* Richler's rendering of Jake's boyhood in Montreal takes into consideration Jake's involvement with his extended family, that is, with parents, uncles, aunts, cousins, and a host of other relatives. In this novel Richler focuses almost exclusively on Joshua's relationship with his strikingly unconventional parents. His father, Reuben, a lovable rogue, is an ex-boxer and petty criminal who delights in making idiosyncratic exegeses of the Bible. His mother, Esther, a very sensual and determined woman, aspires to be a burlesque queen and often rehearses before her young son. Eventually, she leaves Reuben to star in pornographic movies and to open a massage parlor. Joshua initially follows in his father's footsteps: he shoplifts, steals cars, and spends a short time in reform school. As he grows older, he develops an interest in journalism and sets about educating himself and acquiring the necessary experience. Like all Richler's artist-heroes, he makes a pilgrimage to the literary centers of Europe, and at the age of twenty-one, drawn to Spain by his admiration for the heroes of the Spanish Civil War, he settles for a while in Ibiza where he befriends the local Spaniards, experiences the bordellos, and has his first passionate love affair. Impetuous and idealistic like André Bennett of *The Acrobats,* he constantly provokes and challenges a German resident, Dr. Dr. Mueller, whom he presumes to be a Nazi on the run. He vandalizes Mueller's house, and the authorities force him to leave Ibiza.

Joshua flees to London where he befriends Murdoch and woos Pauline, a Canadian senator's daughter, who divorces her vapid husband, Colin Fraser, to marry him. Seven years later they return to Montreal where Joshua establishes himself as an outstanding journalist, a television personality, and the author of *The Volunteers,* a book on the Spanish Civil War. Like Jake Hersh, he is a devoted father and husband. He re-establishes rivalries and friendships with his former schoolmates who are now mostly professionals and businessmen, and he copes with Pauline's Anglo-Canadian society, epitomized by her girlhood friend, Jane Trimble, and her husband, Jack. Into this fairly contented family life intrudes Kevin, a self-centered, unprincipled, forty-year-old adolescent whose fraudulence as a partner in Jack Trimble's stockbroking firm precipitates the crisis of the novel.

Richler includes quite a number of characters and incidents which he cleverly, if mechanically and tangentially, links to the main narrative. The digressive piece on Hollywood, which was published elsewhere as a short story,[25] is a ready instance of this. Richler allows Joshua to visit Hollywood on the pretext of doing an article for his friend, Peabody, an editor of *Playboy.* Little is made of this assignment during or after the trip to Los Angeles. Richler uses the incident primarily to poke fun at the Hollywood establishment: the dinner-table banter, the wheeling and dealing of producers, and the exploitation and prostitution of literary talent. He shows also that Joshua, like himself, is very much the loser's advocate: Joshua treats sympathetically his ailing friend, Murdoch, who is callously discarded by Hollywood manipulators. Despite this function of characterization, the passage would have had no narrative significance if Richler had not tacked it on to the plot by having a photograph taken of Joshua unabashedly kissing a despairing Murdoch, a photograph which is used later seemingly to confirm the rumors of Joshua's homosexuality. Joshua's trip to Cambridge in 1951, again undertaken as a journalistic assignment, is another set piece which offers a comic account of Joshua's affair with an undergraduate and of his first meeting with Murdoch. The extended presentation of his subsequent relationship with Murdoch is tenuously linked to the main narrative through their faked homosexual correspondence which surfaces at the end of the novel.

As in Richler's earlier novels, there are many minor portraits and set pieces, appealing in themselves and sometimes significant to theme and characterization, but not effectively integrated with the main narrative. There are the two extended accounts of the William Lyon Mackenzie King Memorial Society founded by Joshua and his former schoolmates, not to honor but to ridicule the former prime minister. Richler satirizes both Mackenzie King, described as "Mean-spirited, cunning, somewhat demented, and a hypocrite on a grand scale" (160), and the ambitious members of the society who at their annual meetings try to outdo one another in subtly announcing their various achievements, and who snub those with lesser intellectual and cultural attainments; an echo of the Hampstead Heath episode in *St. Urbain's Horseman* is audible here. There are the long, digressive commentaries on London during the Suez crisis, on the Canadian Broadcasting Corporation programming, on the founding of Ottawa, on the changes in Montreal and the effects of the Parti Quebecois victory, on the course of the war between Nationalists and Republicans in Spain, and on the *autos da fé* directed against the Jews. There are Reuben's lively biblical discourses on the Ten Commandments, on Abraham's readiness to sacrifice Isaac, on the Book of Job, and on Esther and Mordecai. (Richler obviously is having fun with his own

name here.) Reuben's discussions are characterized by a raw colloquialism and an ability to apply his interpretation of the Bible to everyday situations:

"God's always needling, testing, his wrath waxing hot. He's a real blow-
hard. Back in Egypt, for instance, when we were in bondage, he could've
got the Hebes paroled with only one plague, but no, after each one he hardened Pharaoh's heart so he could display his whole bag of tricks. And afterwards, once we were sprung, he never once talks to Moses that he doesn't
remind him . . . quote, I am the Lord thy God, which have brought thee
out of the land of Egypt, out of the house of bondage, unquote. Now in
your life if hard times come and you have to borrow money, never take it
from anybody like that, they drive you crazy reminding you every day what
they did for you. I don't care for such types." (86).

In addition to Reuben, who plays a significant role in the narrative
though his discourses are digressive, other fascinating characters have
only the most tenuous links to the plots. Seymour, the compulsive
philanderer, spends his time seducing women while his wife, Molly,
volunteers to comfort the hospitalized sick but mistakes one patient
for another. Richler's inability to resist including comical scenes,
however digressive, is illustrated by his recounting of a puerile trick
played on Seymour by Joshua who mischievously asks a woman he
knows to respond to Seymour's clandestine advertisement for a personal companion. Izzy Singer, the multimillionaire, is portrayed as a
prisoner of his wealth which cannot buy him acceptance by his more
educated schoolmates. Richler includes an amusing but ironical set
piece that shows Izzy at the mercy of his guard dogs and his sophisticated electronic burglar alarm system when he tries to get to his
refrigerator in the middle of the night. Sergeant McMaster has a secondary role in the main narrative, but there are superbly comic
digressions when he discusses with Joshua the manuscript on which
he has been working for ten years. His novel has ten major characters:

"I was going to tell you why ten characters." McMaster sucked in a
mighty puff of his cigarette, his cunning eyes belying his quick smile.
"There's one major character from each province of Canada."
Joshua whistled, impressed. "No one from the Northwest Territories or
the Yukon?"
"Minor."
"If Quebec separates, will you have to revise?" (19)

Joshua's relationship with McMaster is characterized by many such pieces of dialogue which, though they hold up the narration, animate McMaster's character and enliven the novel.

To give shape to this abundance of material, Richler employs an intricate configuration of flashbacks. While the flashbacks in *St. Urbain's Horseman* adhere to a more or less straightforward chronology, in *Joshua Then and Now* rapid and constant shifts back and forth among several time sequences occur. The first two chapters clearly illustrate this. The novel begins with Joshua recuperating from his accident in late spring 1978, then provides a flashback to 1937 when Joshua is six years old. This is followed by a portrait of Joshua just before his accident in early spring 1978. At this point, lonely and depressed since Pauline is ill in hospital, he finds himself surveying his past, thus occasioning many of the flashbacks. The second chapter continues with an account of Joshua's experiences as a boy of twelve, returns to early spring 1978, goes back to Joshua as a boy of eight, advances to 1972, proceeds to early spring 1978, moves back again to 1972, then further back to 1963, goes forward to early spring 1978, recalls Joshua at twenty in 1951, and ends with early spring 1978.

This involved structure demands alertness from the reader. Richler, himself aware of the difficulties the time sequence might pose for the reader, facilitates him, as he did in *St. Urbain's Horseman*, with frequent temporal signposts, constantly mentioning hours, days, weeks, years, and seasons. He introduces almost every episode or incident with such statements as. " Only three weeks earlier" (11), "He was eleven, it was autumn, and ony two months had passed" (13), "In 1963, the year they had returned to Montreal" (31), "at 1 a.m. on an enchanting spring night. . . . 1951 it was" (52), "That was in February, only one week after Pauline had entered the hospital" (75). These copious temporal references make it possible to establish the dates of incidents even when they are not explicitly given. The reader is able to determine, for instance, that the opening scene takes place in late spring, 1978, because Richler indirectly states that Joshua was born in 1931 (59) and that he is currently forty-seven years old (146). The year is verified when it is discovered that Teddy, Joshua's youngest child, was eight years old in June, 1976 (113) and is ten when the novel opens (4). The reference to "Victoria Day" (6), a holiday which falls on the first Monday preceding May 25, confirms that it is late spring.

A few critics have pounced on this involved structure as "needlessly dizzying"[26] and as reflecting "the hasty disorder of a collage."[27] Richler, however, has remarked that he arrived at this structure after much deliberation. The first version of the novel was organized achronologically, but "afraid that the story had just possibly become too confusing for the reader," he attempted "to unravel the whole thing":

. . . I foolishly tried for three or four months to rewrite the novel, setting it in chronological order. Then I realized that I was ruining it. The mysteries were lost. The real relationship of one time to another was being oversimplified. It just didn't work for me. So I abandoned that and I went back to the layered construction.[28]

What does Richler achieve by adopting this layered structure over which he labored so long? And is it really an untidy construction needlessly employed?

The form obviously enabled Richler to avert any likelihood of tedium that could result from a linear chronicling of the experiences of a forty-seven-year-old protagonist. The constant shifting not just among different time sequences but also among different tones, situations, and characters imparts a vibrancy to the novel acknowledged by most reviewers. Richler's structuring also allows him effectively to create suspense, of which the *Times Literary Supplement* says: "I have seldom seen it used more skilfully."[29] As *The Incomparable Atuk, Cocksure,* and *St. Urbain's Horseman* show, this device of suspense (or mystery, to use Richler's term) increasingly becomes a mark of Richler's plotting and structuring. In *St. Urbain's Horseman* he invokes the reader's interest by raising questions in the first chapter about Jake's present predicament which are not answered until late in the novel. In *Joshua Then and Now* a similar structural outline is used, and the reader's curiosity about Joshua's current plight is engaged from the opening page: Why are a senator and an ex-convict on such good terms and together taking stringent measures to protect Joshua? Why have the local and international press suggested that he is a homosexual? Why has Pauline experienced a nervous breakdown and why has she disappeared? Why does Joshua feel that Trimble should put up his estate for sale as an act of contrition? As the novel unfolds, other questions of varying significance to the narrative are raised: Why does Joshua's mother regularly have to take photographs of him? Why are members of the country club so uneasy when Kevin's name is mentioned? Why does Reuben turn pale when Joshua's bar mitzvah is mentioned? Why is Joshua wearing lace panties when Sergeant McMaster visits him? Why does Reuben give Joshua a key to a safety deposit box (which with uncharacteristic lack of curiosity he never opens until two-thirds through the novel)?

Had Richler employed this intricate structure just to achieve a lively and suspenseful narration with no thematic correlation, its use here would have been less easy to justify. However, Richler harnesses the structure to his portrayal of Joshua as a man absorbed with and conscious of the past. In *St. Urbain's Horseman* Jake, in reviewing his life, traces his growth and maturation which are reflected in the more or less straightforward chronological pattern of the flashbacks. In *Joshua Then and Now* it is not—as the title makes us aware—Joshua's development that is explored, but the contrast between what he was and what he is. The episodes are not randomly thrown together but, informed by the organizing principle of contrast between past and present, have a temporal dialectic progression.

Part 4, where the movement to and fro among the various time sequences accelerates, provides perhaps the best illustration of this principle at work. The first chapter relates an incident that occurs at the cottage on Lake Memphremagog while Joshua is recuperating from his accident, and the second tells about an experience at twenty-one on the Balearic island of Ibiza. Richler unobtrusively makes the reader aware of many parallels and differences between the two occasions. In both, Joshua is being questioned by policemen, but while in the present scene he is an assured writer, deferentially treated by Sergeant McMaster, in the Ibiza scene he frantically and futilely tries to persuade Mariano, the Spanish policeman, that he is not guilty of the charges brought against him by Mueller and the others. In both time sequences Joshua has lost someone; however, he is only slightly bothered by the departure of Monique, the girl with whom he has his first passionate affair, while he is now deeply perturbed by Pauline's disappearance. Photographs are important in both episodes: the photograph of Joshua kissing Murdoch, which really reveals the mature Joshua's compassionate nature, falsely helps to label him a homosexual; the alleged photograph of himself and Monique in the nude is used by Mariano to strengthen the case for Joshua's ejection from Spain.

In this Ibiza incident of 1952 Mariano, in response to Joshua's retort that Mueller has accused him falsely of stealing, says: "Everybody is lying but you" (363). In the following chapter which narrates Joshua's meeting with Kevin in the winter of 1977 when Kevin is trying to exonerate himself of fraudulence, Joshua makes a similar response to Kevin and is startled by the "echoes" (368)—a frequent aural image in the novel. In the next chapter, set also in the winter of 1977, Joshua attends Murdoch's funeral in London where he meets Murdoch's son, Ralph, with whose mother he had an adulterous affair in the 1950s; and he is shocked to recognize the parallel between himself and Ed Ryan with whom Joshua's mother in the 1940s had several sexual encounters: "Good grief, he had thought, chilled, I'm his Ed Ryan" (375).

The account of Joshua's ambiguously motivated return to Spain in 1978, twenty-five years after his first visit, is characterized by recurring comparisons between Spain then and now. Richler even underlines the differences between the impoverished Spain of the mid-twentieth century and Spain during its heyday in the seventeenth century. The recounting of Joshua's return to Ibiza is interrupted by a flashback to the philanderer Seymour's recent heart attack, and later by a brief recall of the last meeting of the Mackenzie King Memorial Society whose aging members contrast starkly with young Joshua living in Ibiza of 1952, a place peopled then by the young in one another's arms. The older Joshua's constant thoughts of Pauline, prone to breakdowns and alone in Montreal facing the crisis brought on by her brother's embezzlement, contrasts with the more self-centered concerns of young Joshua. At the end of Chapter 6 Kevin's death is announced, and in the next chapter Joshua, who once deserted Monique and the Friebergs in Ibiza, now feels responsible for Pauline's breakdown since in a sense he abandoned her by going to Spain when she needed him most. Chapter 8 juxtaposes a flashback to Pauline and Joshua's first dinner together with a portrait of her in the hospital, emotionally ill, but perceptively remarking to Joshua: "You are not what you once were" (408).

The concluding chapters of Part 4 include a contrasting study of Uncle Oscar in the 1940s when he is shown thinking up harebrained schemes for becoming a millionaire, and in the 1970s when as an old man he must drive taxis to make a living. There is also an ironic parallel between accounts of the past where young Joshua listens to stories of his father's shady activities, and of the present where seventy-three-year-old Reuben listens to McMaster's report of Joshua's acts of vandalism.

The antithetical arrangement of the various time sequences is not obtrusive, nor is it inflexibly imposed on the novel so as to constrict organic narrative progression and dramatic effectiveness. Mariano's confrontation of Joshua does parallel Joshua's confrontation of Kevin, but Richler is equally anxious in narrating the first to evoke an element of intrigue, and in relating the second to keep the reader guessing (as he does throughout the novel) about whether Kevin is in fact guilty or was used as a scapegoat by Trimble. The flashback to Seymour's heart attack is a richly amusing episode, introduced not just for the contrast between the young and the old, but as comic relief from the detailed portrayal of Joshua's darkening attitude and testy behavior on his return to Spain. The contrasts between Spain then and now are quite evident in Richler's account of the journey through Spain, but he introduces as well Joshua's constant feelings of foreboding about Pauline alone in Montreal to heighten the dramatic effect.

The numerous flashbacks and references to dates and ages are the most prominent indication of Joshua's preoccupation with the past. Other minor motifs and symbols also convey this preoccupation. Richler uses the metaphor of sifting past experiences several times: on one occasion Joshua begins "to sift through cardboard boxes . . . sorting out old papers" (357); on another, he is "sifting through the conundrums of a childhood that still bewildered him" (17). The episode in which characters representing three generations (the Senator and Reuben, Joshua, and his son, Alex) dig up bottles of liquor buried in a coffin since prohibition is symbolic of the exhumation of the past; Richler emphasizes the comic in his narration of this incident, but this does not suppress the archetypal symbolic function of the grave. Likewise, the key Joshua wears around his neck which unlocks a box from the past is plainly symbolic even though it is also a device of suspense.

Throughout the novel Richler shows Joshua constantly measuring what he and others are now by what they once were. On his way to Ibiza during a stopover in London, Joshua muses about this aspect of himself:

And then, looking up the number of an old Fleet Street chum, he suddenly grasped that he couldn't make out the dancing names in the telephone book unless he held the page a good distance away from his eyes. Now I'm going to need reading glasses, he thought.

Wandering down Carlisle Street, he was reminded of those long afternoons that he used to unwind in the Partisan Coffee Bar and of the silly left-wing attitudes they had cherished at the time. Jesus, when he looked back on himself at any age, Joshua then rather than now, it seemed he had always been such a horse's ass. O.K., he was willing to accept that, given his present unquestioned wisdom. But didn't it mean that if he ever reached sixty, he would take himself to have been just as much of an oaf in his late forties? Yes? No? He had no answers. (378)

Such obsessive comparison of now and then reminds Joshua of man's mortality and of the often ironical reversals in human fortunes occasioned by the passage of time. Most important, Joshua's obsession makes him aware of the constricting hold certain past incidents may have on the individual.

If Jake at the age of thirty-seven is conscious in *St. Urbain's Horseman* of growing old, Joshua ten years older is much more aware of this. The epigraph taken from the first stanza of Auden's poem, "Lullaby," introduces the reader to Joshua's concern with ephemerality and mortality, and the many references to Joshua's progressive ages are constant reminders of this. In this novel, unlike *St. Urbain's Horseman*, it is not just the protagonist who confronts aging. Pauline frequently mentions her fading beauty and morbidly dreams of being in her coffin. Joshua's conversations with his literary friends, Peabody and Murdoch, invariably touch on mutability. When he revisits Spain, his former companions cannot avoid talking of decay and death. One of the most poignant reminders of the havoc time wreaks on man is Jake's lament for Barbara, a minor character with just a walk-on role:

Thirty years earlier, on their third date, Joshua had managed to unsnap Barbara's brassiere on a bench in Outremont Park. He was the first, she had assured him. Now, after her mastectomy, she counseled others in the hospital, a volunteer worker.
O Barbara Barbara. (178)

Richler provides three accounts of the Mackenzie King Memorial Society meetings in 1959, in 1967, and in the 1970s. These scenes are certainly satirically effective, but they also serve to show the physical decline of the members. While youthful exuberance characterizes their first reunion and professional rivalry their second, their third is haunted by gloomy reports of colleagues incapacitated by tumors and heart problems.

Up to his forty-seventh year, before his wife's illness and disappearance, Joshua considers himself blessed with good fortune. Once a delinquent living in the slums and snubbed by "better-bred boys" (116), he is now rich and famous and resides in prestigious Westmount. Conversely, some of those who were better off and more promising than Joshua, like Sheldon and Kevin, turn out to be disappointments. Of Sheldon, Joshua says:

> Poor Sheldon had once been the most promising of his generation of Leventhals. An unrecognized Quiz Kid. One day president of the Junior Red Cross; the next, a star on the McGill campus. Stroke, stroke, stroke. Graduating *cum laude,* the family pride. And now, twenty-five years later, his face fleshy but his beard trim, his fingernails manicured, reeking of a leathery cologne, Sheldon was big in storm windows, his father-in-law's business. (399)

Kevin's reversal of fortune is given more extended and dramatic treatment. Born into a distinguished Anglo-Canadian family, primed for statesmanship, and given the best tutors, he develops into a parasite and a cheat.

These reversals of fortunes accent the ironies inherent in human life. But more than this, they point to an unsavory aspect of Joshua's personality: his vindictiveness. When Joshua returns to Montreal as a successful writer, Sheldon asks him and Pauline out to dinner:

> They were, Joshua insisted to Pauline, obliged to go.
> "We are most certainly not obliged to go," she said, "but you're still enough of a boy to want to stick it to him."
> "You should have heard his voice on the phone. Oozing envy. I love it."
> "Vengeance is the Lord's, not yours, Joshua."
> "Dress classy. I want your breeding to show." (29)

At the restaurant Joshua takes perverse pleasure in humiliating Sheldon and his wife. This is just one of the many instances of Joshua's vengeful behavior which persuaded one reviewer to declare that "At times, *Joshua Then and Now* seems a chronicle more of grudges than of grief."[30] Joshua is very much aware of this shortcoming in himself. On one occasion, remembering Sheldon's snobbish behavior as a boy,

Joshua deliberately coldshoulders him only to reprimand himself instantly: "Shapiro, you are indeed an abomination" (399). On another, overcome by anger on recalling the exploitation of the Jews by the Spanish Inquisition, he warns himself not to be "a grudgy type" (190). But such warnings go unheeded. Joshua continues to the end of the novel to take satisfaction from his grudges despite Kevin's death and his wife's illness: he treats Uncle Oscar coldly when riding in his taxi for he could not forget that Uncle Oscar once humiliated his father; he returns to Ibiza to take unspecified revenge on Mueller; and he even gloats at Kevin's misfortune, and resents his wife's sororal concern.

In his extended account of Joshua's two visits to Ibiza Richler provides a perceptive examination of how experiences from the past can torment the individual. Noah Adler experiences this in *Son of a Smaller Hero* when he tries to resist the persuasive Polish orator who seeks to foster in Noah and his friends an atavistic hatred for the persecutors of the Jews. The particular experience from the past that comes back to haunt Joshua is more personal rather than ethnical. According to Joshua's interpretation of his encounter with Mueller in 1952, he behaved in a cowardly manner when he unprotestingly allowed Mueller to run him out of Spain, forcing him to part from Monique and to abandon the Friebergs, two aging Jewish refugees, whose new hotel was to be closed down apparently for poor wiring but really because of their association with Joshua. Joshua cannot shed the memory of his cravenness. Mueller's challenge—"Are you a man or a mouse?"—rings in his ears and induces nightmares in which Joshua struggles to defy his antagonist: "If you think you can rob me of my manhood, you're out of your mind. I'm not running, Mueller. . . . I will not be ashamed. I am a man, not a mouse. Understand?" (185). Memories of this past humiliation surface at the oddest moments. At his son's graduation ceremony, for instance, Teddy's scholarly achievement serves but to remind Joshua of his own discreditable conduct: "*I ran once*, Joshua thought. *Me, your father*" (113). Convinced of his own cowardice, Joshua seeks to implant in his children admiration for heroic figures only to realize that he is burdening them "with his own past" (114).

What Joshua discovers when, after twenty-five guilt-ridden years, he returns to Spain to seek redress from Mueller and to make amends to the Friebergs is that he is a victim of his youthful idealism and romanticism. Young Joshua journeys to Spain and settles in Ibiza because Hemingway, his literary idol, whose heroes do "not lack for *cojones*" (233), made Spain his spiritual home. Spain also is the scene of the heroic struggle of the honorable and dedicated men of the International Brigades, with whom Joshua from the age of eight "for reasons unfathomable to him" (102) was fascinated. Like André Bennett and Norman Price, Joshua virtually deifies these heroes and sees their cause not as "a received political idea" but as "a moral inheritance" and as the last of the "clean causes" (233). The men of the International Brigades provide Joshua with a metaphor for honor, courage, and noble aspirations; and for the longest while these heroes, whose achievements he celebrates in *The Volunteers,* constitute the demanding yardstick by which he judges his confrontation with Mueller and finds himself wanting.

Joshua at twenty-one yearns to follow in the footsteps of his heroes, but there is no civil war in which he can prove himself. His preoccupation with heroism and manhood makes him inflate himself into an avenger of the Jews and Mueller into a monstrous Nazi villain. But Joshua is no Horseman, and Mueller is no Mengele. During the war Mueller worked in a government office in Berlin and never saw the front. He was run out of France not for Nazi atrocities but for assaulting a girl in Nice in 1954. He is not a spy, as Joshua believes, but an eccentric writer of Western novels under the pseudonym of Gus McCabe who occasionally lives out his cowboy fantasies. Joshua persists in his inflated conception of Mueller even after he breaks into Mueller's house and finds "no lampshades made of human skin or unmarked bars of soap lying about" (359), just sentimental photographs of Mueller's family and Western novels, posters, and records.

Mariano, whom Joshua visits on his return to Spain, enables him to see his Ibiza experience in its proper perspective. Now in retirement, Mariano considers the incident that Joshua magnifies to be trivial, and Joshua himself is remembered not as a coward but as a "skinny . . . hot-tempered" (394) yet likable youth. Mueller, Mariano recalls, did not run Joshua out of Spain, but simply gave false statements about Joshua for which he later paid the penalty: "Well, after you left, things changed there for Mueller. The officers felt that he had played dirty" (394). And the Friebergs were not deported; on the contrary, they stayed on and prospered. Joshua comes to realize finally that he has been judging himself too harshly and burdening himself with ill-found guilt. He concludes his stay in Ibiza by visiting the site of Mueller's house which is now an estate, the name of which, "The Don Quixote Estate," Richler evidently uses to suggest that Joshua had been tilting at windmills for twenty-five years. When Joshua saw this name, he "sat down on a rock and laughed until he almost cried" (396). It was his moment of epiphany.

> Back in his hotel room, exhilarated, he poured himself a stiff Scotch. He decided that he would not write a new introduction to *The Volunteers*. That was from another time, another place. Let it rest. (397)

With this resolution, a reborn Joshua returns to his family responsibilities in Montreal. However, though Ibiza does not haunt him as before, he wonders at one point what was achieved by his compulsive return to Spain. He tells himself: *"If not for your unnecessary return to Spain—that stupid self-indulgent trip that was to settle nothing, absolutely nothing—she wouldn't be lying in the hospital now"* (137). Joshua is guilt-stricken here, and perhaps the comment should be taken simply as remorse rather than as an objective assessment of his trip to Spain. Yet this may be the beginning of another inner conflict, for Joshua makes the comment after Pauline angrily tells him that he is not what he once was, and that he is now "a coward" (408) because he refuses to acknowledge that he really wants to devote himself to writing rather than to family life.

Richler extends his study of the possessive power of the past by constructing a parallel between Joshua's obsession with Ibiza and Trimble's with his family background. Though Trimble is Anglo-Canadian, his early life, like Joshua's, was one of poverty and constant struggle. Now married to a socialite and financially powerful, he has carefully concealed his past and created for himself a British upper-middle-class pedigree. When challenged by Joshua, who has some inkling of Trimble's true past, Trimble denies his Canadian origin; but eventually, when he visits Joshua recuperating at Lake Memphremagog, he discloses his hidden past, laying stress on his father's and his own humiliation and degradation at the hands of the rich. Trimble's vehement language and vindictive tone in relating these experiences establish his kinship with another Richlerian malcontent, Harry Stein of *St. Urbain's Horseman*, with whom Jake Hersh sympathizes as does Joshua with Trimble. Joshua points to the cathartic effect of Trimble's acknowledging his past when he informs Reuben that Trimble "had a stone in his shoe and he took it out himself" (434). Richler deliberately places this brief account of Trimble exorcising his past at the very end of the novel evidently to emphasize what Joshua and Trimble have accomplished by juxtaposing their experiences then and now, and what Pauline, who is shown returning to Joshua immediately after Trimble's confessional account of his upbringing, must do about her wrenching memories of Kevin.

Reviewers have differed sharply in their responses to the concluding scene of *Joshua Then and Now* which tells of the reunion of the recuperating couple in the garden of Lake Memphremagog and of their walking back to the house with Joshua supported not by his cane but by Pauline. While some dismiss it as a sentimental happy ending,[31] others defend it: "If the reader thinks back to the Auden epigraph—'Lay your sleeping head, my love / Human on my faithless arm . . .'—the quiet acceptance of the last pages seems less sentimental than resigned. It has the dignity of understatement."[32] The gentle reconciliation—intentionally presented by Richler through the eyes of Reuben, perhaps the least sentimental character of the novel— is an affirmation of Auden's quiet acceptance of man's suffering and mortality, and it emanates organically from Joshua's character and his relationship with Pauline as portrayed throughout the novel. Long before his resolution in Ibiza to devote himself to his family, Joshua has shown himself to be a responsible husband and father; and despite his sardonicism, he rejects with Maimonides the pessimistic view that "there exists more evil than good" (190) and that man is not allowed happiness and prosperity.

In this reunion with Pauline, Richler depicts Joshua as a moral and responsible man who, like Jake Hersh, is ready to pick up the pieces of his life and make an effort to be less self-centered and more accommodating of others. But while this reconciliation is taking place, Joshua's vindictive act of planting stolen money in Seligson's house is unfolding offstage with the certain ruin of Sergeant McMaster. It is difficult to say categorically how Richler intends this antithetical characterization of Joshua. Quite likely he conceives of Joshua as having an inherent duality of character—an aspect of Jake Hersh conveyed through the use of Harry Stein as an alter ego. There are indications of this duality throughout the novel. As a boy, Joshua is both Duddy Kravitz and Noah Adler. He has been to reform school, is prematurely worldly, and can be coarse and vulgar; but he also has literary aspirations, develops a social conscience, corrects his father's grammar, and is embarrassed by his father's conduct. As a man, Joshua is both Jake Hersh and Harry Stein. Pauline considers him to be so moral that even "my father's frightened of you" (409), yet he equals Harry Stein's capacity for vengeful vandalism.

Richler never relates Joshua's acts of vandalism directly or dramatically: there are just hints and insinuations, or reported accounts, such as McMaster's of Joshua's disastrous visit to Seligson's house. Also, Joshua himself never acknowledges responsibility for these vicious deeds. This, taken with the indirect form of narration, allows the possibility that Richler sees Joshua's Steinian acts as originating from the dark side of his psyche, or, as Jung would have said, from his shadow.

It is possible that Richler intends no such interpretation of Joshua's malicious deeds and that (like Virgil's newsletter for epileptics in *The Apprenticeship of Duddy Kravitz*) they are simply inconsistencies and illustrations of Richler's inability to resist a comic set piece even when it jars with his primary characterization, tone, or intention. In the Seligson episode, for instance, how likely is Joshua, who accepts with equanimity the barbs about his reputed homosexuality and has just learnt of Pauline's disappearance, to avenge himself against Seligson, a minor character, simply because he makes insulting comments about Joshua's homosexuality? The episode is certainly comic and necessary for plot development, but is it meant to convey an aspect of Joshua's personality? The same is true of scenes of Joshua's childhood which recall Duddy Kravitz's: often it appears as if Richler introduces many of the episodes as comical interludes rather than as serious studies of Joshua's upbringing. How, for instance, is the reader to take Joshua's mother's striptease at his bar mitzvah? Is she portrayed here as a bizarre mother or a farcical caricature? And are Reuben's sermons indicative of his fatherly concern for Joshua's moral upbringing or are they simply rich comic diversions? The effect of this ambiguity of intention in such scenes is to deprive the novel of the sustained intensity of *St. Urbain's Horseman* where farcical and satirical scenes like the episode with Ormsby-Fletcher and the baseball players on Hampstead Heath are set apart and do not intrude on the study of Jake Hersh.

If Joshua's duality of character is possibly just an accident of technique, his ambivalence is not. As with Richler's other protagonists, it is an ingrained aspect of his psyche. He is both hopeful and nihilistic, moral and malicious, accommodating and sardonic. He alternately accepts and rejects his people; in Ibiza, for instance, he sets himself up as an avenger of the Jews and complains bitterly of the

Spanish persecution of the Jews, yet he responds disdainfully to them: "Jews, Jews, Joshua thought, everywhere I go there are other Jews to advise me. Clutching. Claiming. I probably wouldn't even be safe in Senegal" (195). He is devoted to his wife, yet resentful of her: "Professing great and enduring love, Joshua was astonished at the resentment he had been able to nourish . . . " (136). He is disgusted by the vulgarly rich Izzy, a post-apprenticeship Duddy Kravitz, but he defends Izzy against his intolerant and snobbish colleagues. He both belittles and yearns for his youthful intensity: "And yet, and yet, he thought, even as he disowned this other Joshua, I'd give a good deal for a cup of his enthusiasm right now" (147). These ambivalent responses are not as pervasively examined as are Jake's in *St. Urbain's Horseman*. This, of course, is because Joshua, possessing traits of Duddy Kravitz and Harry Stein, is not as introspective as Jake Hersh; and because *Joshua Then and Now* examines the effects of the past on an individual rather than the doubts and vacillations of an ambivalent mind, with which *St. Urbain's Horseman* is concerned.

The origins of *Joshua Then and Now* and certain parallels between Joshua's and Richler's experiences inevitably invite consideration of the closeness of the author and his protagonist. *Joshua Then and Now* originated with Richler's return to Spain in 1976 after an absence of twenty-five years (to do an introductory essay for a book of photographs on Spain). Richler was accompanied by his wife, a fact which reminds the reader that *Joshua Then and Now* is fictional though based in parts on Richler's experiences. After two weeks in Spain, during which time he revisited Ibiza where, like Joshua, he had lived for a short time in his youth, Richler produced not a travel piece but a very long essay about what Ibiza had once meant to him. For the book of photographs, published as *Images of Spain*,[33] Richler wrote a separate introduction which, though it says much about the geography, history, and customs, is essentially dry, for Richler's more personal responses and his more meaningful visit to Ibiza were removed for inclusion in what was to become *Joshua Then and Now*. He rewrote the longer, personal essay as a memoir of his experiences in Ibiza and London, and later revised this memoir, transforming it into a work written in the first person which was "teetering between a memoir and a novel,"[34] and eventually into its present form where the third person replaces the first person. But elements of the memoir are clearly evident, as Richler himself mentions: "I remember, as Joshua does in my novel, . . . coming on this picture of Franco striding through shelled Madrid—a conqueror. I don't know quite what it meant to me at that time. I don't pretend that I was politically conscious at the age of 8 or 9, but for some reason it did move me."[35]

Though the novel is written in the third person throughout, it is possible to identify three fairly distinct authorial foci of narration: the omniscient, as in the accounts of certain incidents from Joshua's boyhood and in set pieces like Izzy's midnight escapade in his kitchen; a third person point of view with emphasis on Joshua as the central intelligence—which is the primary focus of narration; and a third-person point of view where Richler becomes inseparable from Joshua and there is no perceptible authorial mediating presence, as in passages relating Joshua's sentiments on Ibiza, family life, and writing (about which Joshua speaks more as a novelist than a sports writer).[36] Despite this occasional oneness of author and protagonist, Richler manages to keep a proper aesthetic distance between himself and Joshua.

Even more than *St. Urbain's Horseman, Joshua Then and Now* has a great abundance of characters and situations of which one reviewer says that "a more parsimonious novelist might have spread over several novels."[37] But many of these characters and situations, as well as the setting, the themes, and Joshua's temperament, obsession, and relationships recall the earlier novels: and, for some critics, the introduction of the contemporary Montreal setting, the complex use of flashbacks, and the shifting of thematic emphases are not enough to erase "an acute sense . . . of *déjà vu*."[38] Of this uncomfortable feeling of familiarity, one otherwise favorable reviewer says: "It's as if a rich and unusual body of fictional material had become a kind of prison for a writer who is condemned to repeat himself ever more vehemently and inflexibly."[39] It is not unlikely that Richler is conscious of this element in his work and that he—who so often draws on his own experiences for his novels—is attempting, like Joshua, to liberate himself from a possessive past. His next novel, tentatively entitled "Gursky Was Here,"[40] will provide the answer.

Chapter Six
Conclusion:
The Hooded Fang

Though Richler describes himself as a *serious* novelist and affirms that any serious writer is essentially a moralist, to come to his work for homilies and philosophies is to be disappointed. Richler provides no dogma, no hard and fast axioms. His novels conclude with no formulated wisdom. Though he celebrates the traditional virtues, what concerns him is his protagonists' *process* of discovering the validity of these virtues in a more or less amoral contemporary society and their conflicting desire both to protest against this society and to accommodate themselves to it. It is the journey, fraught with anguish and ambivalence, that fascinates Richler rather than the arrival. All his novels reflect this thematic pattern and bear out Richler's observation that every "serious writer has . . . one theme, many variations to play on it."[1]

As we look back over the novels, the change observed is not so much in the nature of the insights as in form and style. Each novel marks an improvement on, or a step in a different direction from, the preceding one. *Son of a Smaller Hero* tries to shed the derivativeness of *The Acrobats* and to achieve characterization that is psychologically more credible. A *Choice of Enemies* acquires a more disciplined, modulated tone and more objective distancing than *Son of a Smaller Hero*. *The Apprenticeship of Duddy Kravitz* has a technical assurance and a poise that mark the end of Richler's apprenticeship period. The novel exhibits unflagging energy, brilliant dialogue, dramatic scenes, and pervasive humor which accentuates Richler's objectivity, ironic perception, and instinctive humanity. *The Incomparable Atuk* and *Cocksure* bring into relief Richler's talent for farce, satirical grotesquerie, black humor, and his skill in adapting for fiction cinematic techniques such as cuts, montage, and dissolves. *St. Urbain's Horseman* and *Joshua Then and Now* depart from the traditional linear structure, employing a complex pattern of flashbacks to give cohesive form to the host of episodes Richler brings together in these recapitulative works. *St. Urbain's Horseman* also shows Richler for the first time communicating certain major themes through a dominant set of symbols.

Richler's numerous journalistic rebukes and satirical strictures on Canadian culture, the Jewish world, and contemporary values at large have created in the popular imagination an impression of him as an opinionated and cocksure writer. However true this may be of some of his journalistic pieces, it should not influence the reader to prejudge Richler's novels, for in certain obvious ways the creative processes of journalism and of fiction are different. Richler's journalistic appraisals lack the complex, ambivalent, and ironic perception of Richler's fiction. Though there are satirical passages in Richler's novels and though he has created in Star Maker one of the most satirical grotesques in contemporary literature, satire is not the prevailing tone of his *oeuvre*. The novels themselves support Richler's protest against an interviewer describing him as a satirist pure and simple.[2] Such an assessment, Richler observes, ignores his larger concern with the novel of character and with being the loser's advocate more than his castigator. Richler certainly possesses considerable talent for satire, but his ambivalence, reflected in so many of his protagonists with whom he is identifiable and through whose consciousness his novels generally are narrated, fosters an inquiring rather than a censorious approach.

Richler's intensely ambivalent perception of the human condition is what sets him apart from certain writers whom he admires and with whom he could otherwise possibly be linked. He thinks highly of Evelyn Waugh whom he considers to be one of the major writers of this century. However, his fiction does not reflect Waugh's pessimistic belief in the defeat of civilization by the forces of savagery. Jake Hersh of *St. Urbain's Horseman* is fearful of the rebirth of Nazism and is overcome by strong nihilistic and apocalyptic feelings, but this is just one of his many contradictory and vacillating responses and certainly does not constitute a prevailing, categorical attitude. Louis-Ferdinand Céline is another writer Richler admires; and, in certain places, his style closely approximates Céline's firm condensation and his preference for raw, scatological images and for robust colloquialism and slang. However, he veers away from Céline's frighteningly dark vision of mankind's fate.

Richler also regards George Orwell highly, and like Jake Hersh in *St. Urbain's Horseman,* he shares Orwell's skepticism of "anybody's panacea" (308). But though in *Cocksure* Richler portrays the corrupting force of political and financial power, he does not envisage, as does Orwell, the spread of tyranny; nor does he reflect Orwell's perennial brooding bitterness. Richler's protagonists, even though they may be defeated in their endeavors to live by traditional and spiritual values, always retain a measure of optimism. The epigraphs of *St. Urbain's Horseman* and *Joshua Then and Now,* both taken from poems by Auden which speak of showing "an affirming flame" in the face of adversity and of perceiving beauty in mortality, encourage the reader to see the conclusions of the two novels as anything but pessimistic. At the end of *St. Urbain's Horseman* Jake rouses himself from a nightmare to change the final entry in his journal about the death of the Horseman—who functions on one level as a symbol of hope—from "died July 20, 1967, in an air crash" to "presumed dead" (467), and at the end of *Joshua Then and Now* Joshua and Pauline are reconciled and ready to face their overwhelming problems together. Such optimism, however, is nervous and hesitant at best, for Richler and his protagonists are always questioning themselves, rarely giving any firmly conclusive answers.

The black humor of *Cocksure* and certain satirical set pieces echo that of Nathanael West, a satirist who influenced Richler and other writers, such as Terry Southern, with whom Richler associated when he first visited Paris in the early 1950s. Richler's work, however, lacks West's organic and pervasive savage tone, his apocalyptic vision, his nightmarish suffering, and images of brutality and violence, such as Homer stomping a boy to death in *The Day of the Locust* or Miss Lonelyhearts crushing a lamb's head with a stone. The black humor that informs Richler's piece on Virgil's magazine for epileptics in *The Apprenticeship of Duddy Kravitz* is exceptional rather than prevalent in that novel and in Richler's work in general. And even *Cocksure,* when juxtaposed with *Miss Lonelyhearts* or *The Day of the Locust,* as David Myers shows,[3] has as much to do with farce and frivolity as with West's trenchant satire and grotesque imagery.

The Street, Richler's collection largely of published reminiscences of St. Urbain Street, reveals the same ambivalence and mingling of tolerance and censure found in the longer fiction. This is particularly evident in a few pieces which have all the dimensions of short stories. A faintly nostalgic tenderness prevalent in these pieces does not dim Richler's sharp, objective perception of his Jewish community. The stories, which are untitled, are at once pathetic and mordant. One recounts the prolonged illness of a bedridden grandmother. Richler describes the obsessive devotion of her daughter who brings the old lady home and nurses her to the detriment of her family life and her own health. He juxtaposes with implied censure the daughter's dedication with her husband's frustration and anger, and with the indifference of the old lady's other children. Ironically, in censuring their behavior, Richler celebrates (like Noah in *Son of a Smaller Hero* and Jake in *St. Urbain's Horseman* when he returns to Montreal for his father's funeral) the stability and security of Jewish family life. Moreover, Richler subdues whatever censure there is by allowing the disinterested young grandson (evidently a fictional counterpart of Richler) to narrate this incident.

The young narrator is not as disinterested when he relates another story about a sophisticated European Jewish refugee, Herr Bambinger, whom his parents, needing additional income, decide to take in as a tenant. The boy resents Mr. Bambinger from the beginning because he is dislodged from his room to accommodate the new tenant. His resentment grows as Bambinger, though he does not "pontificate about what a dull, uncultured country Canada was" like other European refugees,[4] nevertheless makes life miserable for the twelve-year-old narrator by insisting, with the approval of the boy's parents, that he should pay attention to his studies and to his table manners. Yet the narrator exhibits parallel feelings of sympathy for the lonely refugee. When Mr. Bambinger eventually is to be reunited with his family from whom he was separated in Europe during the war, the narrator offers some of his comic books to Bambinger for his young son—a kindly gesture which Bambinger snubs. Soon after, Bambinger learns that his wife and son are lost at sea. Grief-stricken, he decides to vacate his room and caustically tells the boy he can have his bed back: "You've been deprived of a lot. You've suffered a good deal. Haven't you? *Little bastard*" (77). The boy responds with fear and guilt rather than with resentment and anger. His mixed feelings for Bambinger surface in the brief concluding scene. Two weeks after Bambinger learns of the death of his wife and son, the boy sees Bambinger walking toward him on a downtown street. Bambinger, fashionably dressed, is escorting an attractive young lady. "At first I intended to ask him if he was ever going to come round for the stuff in the shed but I crossed to the other side of the street before he spotted me" (77). The conjunction "but" here points up the antithetical response of the narrator: his initial desire to embarrass and reprimand Bambinger by his presence, and his simultaneous tolerance of human frailty when he decides to cross the street to avoid confronting Bambinger.

The experiences of another tenant, Mervyn Kaplansky, an aspiring writer, are also given through the narrator's receptive consciousness. Mervyn's involvement with the boy's parents and their community provides him with an education in sudden shifts of feelings and allegiances in human relationships. Initially, the father, earthy and practical, sees Mervyn as a parasite. In response to this, Mervyn, more a writer by desire than by achievement, mouths all the romantic catchwords about the artist: ". . . it's difficult for an artist to earn a living. Society is naturally hostile to us . . . *I'm* in rebellion against society" (99). The mother, conversely, from the beginning is devoted to this artist who shuns material things. When the father discovers that Mervyn has written a pornographic story under a pseudonym, he warms toward him, proudly taking him to meet his cronies, while the mother begins to resent Mervyn and to doubt his talent. But when she learns that he has sent off a *serious* novel to the publisher, she is once more proud of him as are the other members of the community. Their pride turns to mockery, however, when Mervyn's novel is rejected. Soon after, Mervyn regains their confidence and devotion when, before he flees his community, he lies about getting his novel accepted by a reputable publisher.

In this story the boy functions essentially as an observant, curious narrator. His own response to Mervyn is not stressed save his initial reaction that Mervyn "was the first writer I had ever met and I worshipped him. So did my mother" (93). And he proceeds to analyze his mother's rather than his attitude to Mervyn. The aspect of the boy on which Richler focuses is his growing awareness of the complexity of human relationships. He is struck, for instance, by his father's mixed reaction to Mervyn's curtness to his mother: "My father seemed both dismayed and a little pleased that someone had spoken up to my mother" (104). And, on another occasion, he is surprised to discover that there is another side to his father's gruffness and taciturnity: "Listening to him, his tender tone with Mervyn and the surprise of his laughter, I felt that I had reason to be envious. My father had never talked like that to me or my sister. But I was so astonished to discover this side of my father, it was all so unexpected, that I

soon forgot my jealousy" (109). Incidentally, this story is presented
as memoir, and it is interesting to speculate on the possible influence
Mervyn had on Richler's own decision to become a writer.

The boy's mixed response to his father here is no different from
that of Noah of *Son of a Smaller Hero* and Jake of *St. Urbain's Horseman*
to their similarly earthy fathers, who, robbed of much of their self-
esteem by socially-conscious wives, become progressively unsure of
themselves in their relationship with their artistically inclined sons.
The filial theme, just a minor concern of these two novels, emerges
through incidents remembered in the main on the deaths of the protagonists' fathers, and, as such, it is informed chiefly by the softening
tone of fond remembrance. But the fondness cannot hide or disguise
the patently strained and guarded relationship between sons and fathers which blows warm and cool from one paragraph to another,
from one recalled incident to the next.

In *St. Urbain's Horseman* Richler, for the first time, portrays his
protagonist in the reverse role of father. He gives no more emphasis
to this aspect of Jake's character than he does to Jake's filial experience, yet Jake's sporadic thoughts of his children, particularly of
Sammy, his eldest son, reveal the same doubts and uneasiness that
govern his relationship with others. Sammy makes him aware of one
of the ironies in his life: as a boy in Montreal, Jake was ashamed of
his parents' Yiddish accent; now his son, born and living in London,
mocks Jake's "immigrant's twang" (6). On one occasion, Jake writes
a playful coded message for his son, adding a postscript that sons
should love their fathers. He inserts the letter in Sammy's notebook,
but immediately after "enraged with himself, he suddenly, savagely,
retrieved it," adding self-reprimandingly: "Leave the kid alone, don't
bug him" (11). On another occasion, wondering how to tell Sammy
that he is likely to be jailed for his alleged sexual crimes, Jake
inexplicably recalls his own empty relationship with his father:
"What do you say to him? I never got to know my father and now
it's too late. Or, look here, starting next week I may be a boarder at
Dartmoor for a while" (42). At the end of the novel, as Jake wrestles
with his chronic uncertain feelings and sets about picking up the
pieces of his shattered life, one of his resolutions concerns his children: "He resolved to be good to Sammy when he came home from
school. Molly wouldn't irritate him today" (461). In *Joshua Then and
Now* Joshua, who also has had very mixed feelings as a boy toward
his father, does not want to be bothered by his children, yet is wor-

ried that his eldest child may not like him "any more" and wonders whether he is "an inadequate father" (101).

In *Jacob Two-Two Meets the Hooded Fang*[5] Richler formulates Jake's and Joshua's mixed responses to their children in the patently ambivalent and memorable character, the Hooded Fang. This fanciful children's novel allows itself to be read on two levels. On the first, intended clearly for children, the novel is about the wish fulfillment of an incompetent child who dreams of performing heroic deeds in which his family takes pride. Jacob, six years old, frustrated by his inability to ride bicycles, whistle, dial telephone numbers, write cursive, or catch a ball, is taken to court and tried (in a dream sequence which echoes *Alice in Wonderland*) for his incompetence and unintentional rudeness to an adult. He is sentenced to a prison filled with equally incompetent children and run by a horrible keeper, the Hooded Fang. Jacob, discovering that the Hooded Fang is really softhearted and only pretends to be menacing, manages to set himself and the other inmates free, thus earning the respect of his older brothers and sisters. As in his adult novels, Richler employs fast-paced narration and lively incremental dialogue. He creates for children a scary atmosphere through his diction and imagery: the children's prison is on an island aptly named Slimer's Isle, which is shrouded by perpetual fog and infested with snakes, crocodiles, wolverines with yellow snaggle teeth, millions of deathwatch beetles, and quicksand.

The novel also invites reading at a deeper level. Richler, adhering to his credo of being the loser's advocate, makes the reader aware of the vulnerability and insecurity of the young child when ignored or misunderstood, unintentionally or otherwise, by adults, and of the child's anger and frustration which surface in dreams of vengeance against grown-ups. Richler has mentioned that his own adolescent affection for superheroes of comic books has something to do with seeing them as "revenge figures against what seemed a gratuitously cruel adult world."[6] He balances this sympathetic portrayal of the child with an equally understanding depiction of the Hooded Fang, an embodiment of the duality of the adult, or more precisely of the father, who must be both stern and loving. Jacob discovers that behind the Hooded Fang's apparent meanness and harshness, there is a gentler soul, reluctant to show itself openly, yet evident in the many little acts of charity and love. To say that the Hooded Fang's ambivalence toward Jacob derives from the paternal experience of Richler—

who, incidentally, has said that "I don't want to be my son's friend, I want to be his father. I'd like to be his friend, too, when he's older, perhaps. . ."[7]—would be speculation, however informed. But to state that this aspect of the Hooded Fang is indicative of Richler's inherent vision of the human condition in his fiction would be an accurate assessment of Richler the novelist.

Notes and References

Chapter One

1. Eugene Bleuler, *Dementia Praecox, or the Group of Schizophreniacs* (1911; New York: International University Press, 1950). Bleuler, Freud, and other psychiatrists and psychologists consider ambivalence in general as a source of undesirable stress. In literature, however, we regard a writer's ambivalence favorably since it *could* encourage a more comprehensive perspective of experience and *could* become a source of enriching complexity, subtlety, and tension, particularly when effectively communicated by such rhetorical devices as ambiguity, irony, antithesis, and paradox, or by stimulating inconsistency, indecisiveness, and contradiction in determining characterization, narrative, tone, and structure. It should be noted that William Empson includes confusion and contradiction in a literary work among his seven types of ambiguity, but more or less restricts this to *verbal* confusion and contradiction. He describes ambiguity as "any *verbal* nuance, however slight, which gives room for alternative reactions to the same *piece of language*" (*Seven Types of Ambiguity,* London: Chatto & Windus, 1930, p. 1. Emphasis added). Confusion and contradiction in structure or plot, for instance, fall outside his definition; consequently, maintaining a distinction between ambiguity, as defined by Empson, and these other rhetorical means of communicating a writer's ambivalent vision is necessary.

2. Graeme Gibson, *Eleven Canadian Novelists* (Toronto, 1973), p. 270.

3. Mordecai Richler, *Shovelling Trouble* (Toronto, 1972), p. 20; hereafter cited in the chapter as *ST* with page number in parentheses. Having described himself as a "serious" novelist, Richler proceeds to add: ". . . I would say that any serious writer is a moralist and only incidently [*sic*] an entertainer."

4. Mordecai Richler, *The Street* (Toronto, 1969), p. 8.

5. "Q for Quest," Box 32, Mordecai Richler Papers, University of Calgary Library.

6. Richler, *The Street,* p. 8.

7. Ibid., pp. 10–11.

8. Ibid., p. 26.

9. Mordecai Richler, "Shades of Darkness," *Points,* no. 8 (December 1950), pp. 30–34.

10. Mordecai Richler, "Like Children to the Fair," in Timothy O'Keeffe, ed., *Alienation* (London: McGibbon & Kee, 1960), p. 164.

11. See, for instance, interview with Keith Ashwell, *Edmonton Journal* (13

March 1970), p. 71; and Press Release on the movie, *The Apprenticeship of Duddy Kravitz*, Mordecai Richler Papers, Box 5, University of Calgary Library.

12. Interview with William Foster, *Scotsman* (24 September 1971), p. 26.

13. Interview with Ian MacDonald in *Saturday Gazette* (6 April 1974), p. 45.

14. See, for instance, his comments in "Playing the Circuit," in David Weisstub, ed., *Creativity and the University* (Toronto: York University, 1975), pp. 9–28.

15. Mordecai Richler, "Manny Moves to Westmount," *Saturday Night* 92 (January 1977): 29–36.

16. Interview with Marilyn Beker, *Montreal Gazette* (2 June 1971), p. 12.

17. Personal interview with Mordecai Richler, Montreal, 23 October 1978.

18. Mordecai Richler, "The Universe of Hatred," *Spectator* (2 September 1966), pp. 290–91.

19. See, Victor Ramraj, "Diminishing Satire: A Study of V.S. Naipaul and Mordecai Richler," in C.D. Narasimhaiah, ed., *Awakened Conscience: Studies in Commonwealth Literature* (New Delhi, 1978), pp. 261–74.

20. V.S. Naipaul, *The Middle Passage* (London: Andre Deutsch, 1962), p. 5.

21. Interview, *Inner Space,* Carleton University, Ottawa (19 February 1969), n.p.

22. Interview with Keith Ashwell, *Edmonton Journal,* p. 71.

23. T.S. Eliot, *Selected Essays* (London: Faber, 1932), p. 18.

24. Mordecai Richler, *The Acrobats* (London, 1970), p. 67.

25. Mordecai Richler, *Son of a Smaller Hero* (Toronto, 1966), p. 169.

26. Budd Schulberg, *What Makes Sammy Run* (New York: Random House, 1941; 1952); Harold Robbins, *A Stone for Danny Fisher* (New York: Knopf, 1952).

27. Interview with Marci McDonald, *Calgary Herald Magazine* (25 November 1973), p. 7.

28. Nathan Cohen, "A Conversation with Mordecai Richler," in David Sheps, *Mordecai Richler* (Toronto, 1971), p. 38.

29. Ibid., p. 42. Richler says: "I am poor on construction, and am willing to take criticism and suggestions."

30. Mordecai Richler, *Hunting Tigers Under Glass* (Toronto, 1968), p. 85.

31. Ibid., p. 87.

32. Interview, *Inner Space,* n. p.

33. Donald Cameron, *Conversations with Canadian Novelists II* (Toronto, 1973), p. 116.

34. Leslie Fiedler, "Some Notes on the Jewish Novel in English," *Running Man* 1 (July–August 1968): 20.

Chapter Two

1. Mordecai Richler, *Shovelling Trouble,* p. 19.
2. Desmond Pacey, *Creative Writing in Canada* (Toronto: Ryerson, 1971), p. 265.
3. John Metcalf, for instance, sees sentimentality as one of Richler's "more endearing frailties" in *Spectator* (15 July 1955), p. 105. On the other hand, Gershon Baruch in *Bulletin* (November 1955) is repelled by Richler's harshness. Richler responds to such divergent views in *Hunting Tigers Under Glass* (Toronto, 1968), p. 9.
4. Mordecai Richler, *Son of a Smaller Hero* (Toronto, 1966), p. 203; hereafter page references cited in parentheses in the text.
5. Interview with Gibson, *Eleven Canadian Novelists,* pp. 287–288.
6. V.S. Pritchett, "Climacteric," *New Statesman* 65 (31 May 1963):832.
7. Interview with Nathan Cohen, in Sheps, *Mordecai Richler,* p. 32.
8. Mordecai Richler, *The Apprenticeship of Duddy Kravitz* (Harmondsworth, 1964), p. 48; hereafter page references cited in parentheses in the text.
9. Interview with Gibson, *Eleven Novelists,* p. 279.
10. Bernard Schilling, *The Comic Spirit* (Detroit: Wayne State University Press), p. 147.
11. A. R. Bevan, for instance, is critical of Duddy in "The Apprenticeship of Duddy Kravitz" (in Sheps, *Mordecai Richler,* p. 88), while Warren Tallman's "The Wolf in the Snow" is favorable to him (Ibid., pp. 78–83). Incidentally, in Ted Kotcheff's film version of the novel, scripted by Richler, Duddy is favorably portrayed, an interpretation of him that robs the movie of the absorbing tension of the novel.
12. William New, "The Apprenticeship of Discovery," in Sheps, *Mordecai Richler,* p. 71.
13. John Ferns, "Sympathy and Judgment in Mordecai Richler's *The Apprenticeship of Duddy Kravitz," Journal of Canadian Fiction* 3 (Winter 1974): 78.
14. Interview with Gibson, *Eleven Novelists,* p. 290.
15. Ibid.
16. See, for instance, D. J. Dooley, *Moral Vision in the Canadian Novel* (Toronto, 1979), p. 106.
17. Interview with Gibson. *Eleven Novelists,* p. 280.

Chapter Three

1. Mordecai Richler, interview with Gibson, *Eleven Canadian Novelists,* pp. 289–90.
2. Letter to Robert Gottlieb, 16 February 1954, Box 53, Mordecai Richler Papers.
3. Mordecai Richler, *The Acrobats* (London, 1970), pp. 39–40; hereafter page references cited in parentheses in the text.

4. Letter to Robert Gottlieb, 16 February 1954.

5. "Q for Quest," Box 32, Mordecai Richler Papers.

6. Ibid.

7. Letter to Robert Gottlieb, 16 February 1954.

8. Nathan Cohen, "Heroes of the Richler View," in David Sheps, *Mordecai Richler* (Toronto, 1971), p. 53.

9. Interview with Gibson, *Eleven Novelists,* p. 290.

10. George Bowering, "And the Sun Goes Down," in Sheps, *Mordecai Richler,* p. 12.

11. Mordecai Richler, *Shovelling Trouble* (Toronto, 1972), p. 15.

12. Joyce Werner's letter, 7 July 1957, Box 57, Mordecai Richler Papers.

13. Mordecai Richler, interview, *Book and Bookmen* (April 1957), p. 40.

14. Mordecai Richler, interview with Nathan Cohen, in Sheps, *Mordecai Richler,* p. 40. In *A Choice of Enemies* Norman expresses the same idea in similar phrases: ". . . the argument was not one of principle but of power" (p. 106).

15. Mordecai Richler, *A Choice of Enemies* (Toronto, 1977), p. 62; hereafter page references cited in parentheses in the text.

16. Interview with Gibson, *Eleven Novelists,* p. 284.

17. Ibid., p. 290.

18. Bruce Stovel, Introduction to *A Choice of Enemies* (Toronto, 1977), p. xiv.

19. Kerry McSweeney, "Revaluing Mordecai Richler," in *Studies in Canadian Literature* 4 (Summer 1979): 124.

20. Nathan Cohen, "Heroes of the Richler View," p. 55.

21. Stovel, Introduction, p. vii.

22. It is worth noting that a more mature Richler has stated of a fellow novelist: "MacLennan's characters seem to be fabricated of points-of-view rather than flesh and blood" (*Hunting Tigers Under Glass,* p. 19).

Chapter Four

1. Mordecai Richler, *The Incomparable Atuk* (Toronto, 1971), p. 30; hereafter page references cited in parentheses in the text.

2. George Woodcock, *Mordecai Richler* (Toronto, 1970), p. 44.

3. Malcolm Ross, Introduction to *The Incomparable Atuk,* p. x.

4. F. W. Watt, "Letters in Canada: Fiction," *University of Toronto Quarterly* 33 (July 1964): 390.

5. Granville Hicks, *Saturday Review* 46 (24 August 1963): 37.

6. Mordecai Richler, Interview with John Metcalf, *Journal of Canadian Fiction* 3 (Winter 1974): 74.

7. John Ferns, *Journal of Canadian Fiction* 3 (Winter 1974): 82. See also David Segal's review, *New Republic* (12 October 1963), p. 27.

8. Compare with Richler's "I was . . . a writer who merely happened to be Jewish." *Hunting Tigers Under Glass,* p. 9.

9. Interview with Nathan Cohen, in Sheps, *Mordecai Richler,* p. 23.

10. W. F. Gavin, review of *Stick Your Neck Out, America* 109 (7 September 1963): 244.

11. Woodcock, *Mordecai Richler,* p. 53.

12. Mordecai Richler, *Cocksure* (Toronto, 1968), p. 142; hereafter page references cited in parentheses in the text.

13. Interview with Donald Cameron, *Conversations with Canadian Novelists II* (Toronto, 1973), p. 119.

14. Mordecai Richler, "James Bond Unmasked," *Commentary* 46 (July 1968): 77–81.

15. Mordecai Richler, "Mortimer Griffin, Shalinsky, and How They Settled the Jewish Question," *Tamarack Review,* no. 7 (Spring 1958), pp. 30–45.

16. Philip Toynbee, review of *Cocksure, London Magazine* (May 1968), p. 79.

17. Desmond Pacey, review of *Cocksure, Fiddlehead* 77 (Summer 1968): 89.

18. Interview with Cameron, *Conversations,* p. 119.

19. Ibid., p. 117.

20. These comments are taken respectively from: review, *Time* 91 (8 March 1968): 98; Marian Engel, review, *New York Times Book Review* (5 May 1968), p. 37; David Haworth, review, *New Statesman* 75 (19 April 1968): 520.

21. *Times* (London) *Literary Supplement* (16 May 1968), p. 497.

22. Toynbee, review of *Cocksure,* p. 79.

23. Interview with Cameron, *Conversations,* p. 117.

24. Harold Hart, ed., *Summerhill: For and Against* (New York: Hart, 1970), p. 17.

25. Mordecai Richler, *Shovelling Trouble,* p. 36.

Chapter Five

1. Mordecai Richler, *St. Urbain's Horseman* (Toronto, 1971), p. 21; hereafter page references cited in parentheses in the text.

2. Concerning the process of creating the two novels, Richler has stated: "Riding into my second year on *St. Urbain's Horseman* . . . I finally got stuck so badly that there was nothing for it but to shove the manuscript aside. I started in on another novel, a year's heat, which yielded *Cocksure.*" See *Shovelling Trouble,* p. 14. Elsewhere, he has observed that *Cocksure* "sort of unblocked" him when he could make no headway with *St. Urbain's Horseman.* See interview with John Metcalf, *Journal of Canadian Fiction* 3 (Winter 1974): 74.

3. Interview with Donald Cameron, in *Conversations with Canadian Novelists,* p. 121.

4. Mordecai Richler, "London Province," *Encounter* 19 (July 1962):40–44.

5. Richler, "The Holocaust and After," *Shovelling Trouble*, pp. 84–96.

6. Richler, "This Year in Jerusalem," *Hunting Tigers Under Glass*, pp. 130–60.

7. Mordecai Richler, "Dinner with Ormsby-Fletcher," *New American Review*, no. 1 (September 1967), pp. 70–80; "Playing Ball on Hampstead Heath," *Gentleman's Quarterly* (August 1966), pp. 90, 140, 142–48; "How They Sell Canada to the Right Kind of Immigrants," *Maclean's* (2 December 1963), p. 80.

8. Interview with Nathan Cohen, in David Sheps, *Mordecai Richler*, p. 23.

9. Robert Brandeis, "Up from St. Urbain's," *Jewish Dialogue* (Summer 1973), p. 47; Warren Tallman, "Need for Laughter," *Journal of Canadian Literature*, no. 56 (Spring 1973), p. 73; David Sheps, "Waiting for Joey: the Theme of the Vicarious in *St. Urbain's Horseman*," *Journal of Canadian Fiction* 3 (Winter 1974): 88; Donald Cameron, "Aren't we all Made of Flesh?" *The Nation* 212 (14 June 1971): 760; Wilfred Cude, "The Golem as Metaphor for Art," *Journal of Canadian Studies* 12 (Spring 1977): 51.

10. Of his allusion to Aaron, Richler has stated in an interview with John Metcalf, *Journal of Canadian Fiction* 3 (Winter 1974); 76: "No one seems to realise that the Horseman is a Golden Calf that [Jake's] made for himself."

11. Mordecai Richler, "St. Urbain's Horseman," *Tamarack Review*, no. 41 (Autumn 1966), pp. 137–42, 145–50.

12. Mordecai Richler Papers, Box 14, University of Calgary Library.

13. Interview with John Metcalf, *Journal of Canadian Fiction*, p. 73.

14. Mordecai Richler, "A With-It Professor . . . ," *Saturday Night* (February 1969), pp. 45–46.

15. William Foster, "The Return of Mordecai Richler," *Scotsman* (24 September 1971), p. 23.

16. Richler, *Shovelling Trouble*, p. 84.

17. Cameron, *Conversations*, p. 125.

18. Ibid., p. 124.

19. See Richler's television adaptation of this play, "The Fall of Mendel Krick," Box 34, Mordecai Richler Papers.

20. F. Scott Fitzgerald, *The Last Tycoon* (New York: Scribner's, 1940; 1924), p. 74.

21. Alberto Gerchunoff, *Los Gauchos Judios* (Buenos Aires: University of Buenos Aires Press, 1964).

22. Leslie Fiedler, "Master of Dreams," *Partisan Review* (Summer 1967), pp. 339–56. In an interview with the present writer (23 October 1979) Richler said that he did not recall reading this essay. In "Huckleberry Flintstone" Richler mentions another essay by Fiedler, "Race—the Dream & the

Nightmare," in *Commentary* (October 1963), pp. 297–304. Of this essay, Richler says in *Shovelling Trouble*, p. 105: Fiedler deals "perceptively, freshly, with real and imagined racial myths and guilt" in American society.

23. Robert Alter, "Jewish Dreams and Nightmares," *Commentary* 45 (January 1968): 54.

24. Mordecai Richler, *Joshua Then and Now* (Toronto, 1980), p. 113; hereafter page references cited in parentheses in the text.

25. Mordecai Richler, "Joshua in Hollywood," *Chatelaine* 53 (May 1980): 50–1, 118–27.

26. Thomas Edwards, review, *New York Times Book Review* 85 (22 June 1980): 11.

27. George Woodcock, review in *World Literature Written in English* 20 (Spring, 1981): 94.

28. Interview with Walter Goodman, *New York Times Book Review* 85 (22 June 1980): 22.

29. David Lodge, review, *Times* (London) *Literary Supplement* (26 September 1980), p. 1056.

30. Betty Falkenberg, review, *New Leader* 63 (11 August 1980): 25.

31. See, for instance, George Woodcock, review in *WLWE*, p. 93, and Nancy Hoffman, review in *Commonweal* 107 (21 November 1980): 668.

32. Betty Falkenberg, review, *New Leader*, p. 25.

33. Mordecai Richler and Peter Christopher, *Images of Spain* (Toronto, 1977).

34. Interview with Walter Goodman, *New York Times Book Review*, p. 22.

35. Ibid., p. 11.

36. Joshua and the novelist Murdoch, for instance, discuss whether they are "artificers" or "liars" (284); and Murdoch's son tells Joshua that Joshua and Murdoch wrote "about how groovy it was to be born poor" (277).

37. David Lodge, review, *Times* (London), p. 1056.

38. George Woodcock, review, *WLWE*, p. 93.

39. Thomas Edward, review, *New York Times Book Review*, p. 25.

40. Editorial Note, *Saturday Night* (January–February 1977), p. 8.

Chapter Six

1. Mordecai Richler, *Shovelling Trouble*, p. 19.

2. Earle Toppings, "Mordecai Richler: Interview," *Canadian Writers on Tape* (Toronto: O.I.S.E., 1970).

3. David Myers, "Mordecai Richler as Satirist," *A Review of International English Literature* 4 (January, 1973): 47–61.

4. Mordecai Richler, *The Street*, p. 71; hereafter page references cited in parentheses in the text.

5. Mordecai Richler, *Jacob Two-Two Meets the Hooded Fang* (Toronto, 1975).

6. Mordecai Richler, *Hunting Tigers Under Glass*, p. 73.

7. Quoted in George Anthony's review of *St. Urbain's Horseman, Toronto Telegram*, 5 June 1971, p. 35.

Selected Bibliography

PRIMARY SOURCES

1. Books

The Acrobats. Toronto: Ambassador, 1954; London: Deutsch, 1954; New York: Putnam, 1954; London: Sphere, 1970.

Son of a Smaller Hero. Toronto: Collins, 1955; London: Deutsch, 1955; New York: Paperback Library, 1965; Toronto: M & S, 1966.

A Choice of Enemies. Toronto: Collins, 1957; London: Deutsch, 1957. London: Quartet, 1973; Toronto: M & S, 1977.

The Apprenticeship of Duddy Kravitz. Toronto: Collins, 1959; London: Deutsch, 1959; Boston: Little Brown, 1959; Toronto, M & S, 1969; Harmondsworth: Penguin, 1964.

The Incomparable Atuk. Toronto: McClelland and Stewart, 1963; London: Deutsch, 1963; Toronto: M & S, 1971; as *Stick Your Neck Out,* New York: Simon and Schuster, 1963.

Cocksure. Toronto: McClelland and Stewart, 1968; London: Weidenfeld and Nicolson, 1968; New York: Simon and Schuster, 1968; New York: Bantam, 1971.

Hunting Tigers Under Glass: Essays and Reports. Toronto: McClelland and Stewart, 1968; London: Weidenfeld and Nicolson, 1969. London: Panther, 1971.

The Street: A Memoir. Toronto: McClelland and Stewart, 1969; London: Weidenfeld and Nicolson, 1972; London: Panther, 1971.

Canadian Writing Today, ed. Harmondsworth: Penguin, 1970.

St. Urbain's Horseman. Toronto: McClelland and Stewart, 1971; London: Weidenfeld and Nicolson, 1971; New York: Knopf, 1971; New York: Bantam, 1972.

Shovelling Trouble. Toronto: McClelland and Stewart, 1972; London: Quartet, 1973.

Notes on an Endangered Species and Others. New York: Knopf, 1974. (Most of these essays appear in *Shovelling Trouble.*)

Jacob Two-Two Meets the Hooded Fang. Toronto: McClelland and Stewart, 1975; London: Deutsch, 1975; New York: Knopf, 1975; New York: Bantam, 1977.

Images of Spain (with Peter Christopher). Toronto: McClelland and Stewart, 1977. (A volume of photographs with text by Richler.)

Joshua Then and Now. Toronto: McClelland and Stewart, 1980; New York: Knopf, 1980; London: Macmillan, 1980.

2. Mordecai Richler Papers

The Mordecai Richler Papers (to 1973). Special Collections, University of Calgary Library, Calgary, Alberta, Canada.

3. Articles and Stories

Note: Richler has collected several of his numerous published articles and stories in *Hunting Tigers Under Glass, The Street, Shovelling Trouble,* and *Notes on an Endangered Species and Others.* What follows is a selected list of other published pieces.

"Shades of Darkness." *Points,* no. 8 (December 1950), pp. 30–34.

"Secret of the Kugel: Story." *New Statesman and Nation* 52 (15 September 1956): 305–06.

"Wally Sylvester's Canadiana." *Tamarack Review,* no. 17 (August 1960), pp. 37–42.

"Like Children to the Fair." *Alienation.* Edited by Timothy O'Keefe. London: MacKibbon & Kee, 1960, pp. 158–67.

"Red Menace: Story." *New Statesman* 62 (22 September 1961): 380–82.

"Some Grist for Mervyn's Mill: Story." *Kenyon Review* 24 (Winter 1962): 80–105.

"Playing Ball on Hampstead Heath." *Gentleman's Quarterly* (August 1966), pp. 90, 140, 142–48.

"St. Urbain's Horseman: Story." *Tamarack Review,* no. 41 (Autumn 1966), pp. 137–142, 145–150.

"Dinner with Ormsby-Fletcher." *New American Review* 1 (September 1967): 70–80.

"This Year at the Arabian Nights Hotel." *Tamarack Review,* no. 47 (Spring 1968), pp. 9–18.

"A Liberal Education: Story." *Paris Review* 11 (Winter 1968): 55–63.

"Uncertain World." *Canadian Literature,* no. 41 (Summer 1969), pp. 23–27.

"Love Affair: Story: Excerpt from *St. Urbain's Horseman.*" *McCall's* 98 (January 1971): 92–94.

"Greening of Hersh: Excerpt from *St. Urbain's Horseman.*" *Chatelaine* 44 (May 1971): 38–39, 58–60.

"Canada: an Immensely Boring Country Until Now." *Life* 70 (9 December 1971): 54–62.

"Playing the Circuit." *Creativity and the University.* Edited by David N. Weisstub. Toronto: York University, 1975, pp. 8–28.

"Manny Moves to Westmount: Story." *Saturday Night* 92 (January 1977): 29–36.

"Oh! Canada! Lament for a Divided Country." *Atlantic* 240 (December 1977): 41–55.

"Writing Jacob Two-Two." *Canadian Literature,* no. 78 (Autumn 1978), pp. 6–8.

"Joshua Then and Now: An Excerpt." *Tamarack Review,* no. 80 (Spring 1980), pp. 5–31.

4. Selected Film, Television, and Radio Scripts
"The Trouble with Benny." Television adaptation of Richler's story. Britain ITV, 1959.
"Q for Quest." Television programme featuring excerpts from Richler's fiction. Canada: CBC, 1961.
"The Fall of Mendel Krick." Television adaptation of Isaac Babel's "Sunset." Canada: CBC, 1963.
"It's Harder to be Anybody." Radio adaptation of Richler's story. BBC, CBC, 1964.
Life at the Top. Film based on a novel by John Braine. Romulus, 1965.
"The Bells of Hell." Television play. Canada: CBC, 1974. A French translation of this script has been published as *Les Cloches D'Enfer.* Ottawa: Leméac, 1974.
The Apprenticeship of Duddy Kravitz. Film based on Richler's novel. Paramount, 1974.
"The Wordsmith." TV adaptation of Richler's story. Canada: CBC, 1979.

SECONDARY SOURCES

Bevan, A. R. Introduction to *The Apprenticeship of Duddy Kravitz.* Toronto: McClelland and Stewart, 1969, pp. 5–8.
Birbalsingh, Frank. "Mordecai Richler and the Jewish-Canadian Novel." *Journal of Commonwealth Literature,* 7 (June 1972): 72–82. Provides an appraisal of Richler's novels up to *Cocksure.*
Bowering, George. "And the Sun Goes Down: Richler's First Novel." *Canadian Literature,* no. 29 (Summer 1966), pp. 7–17. Evaluates *The Acrobats,* pointing out echoes of Hemingway.
Brandeis, Robert. "Up From St. Urbain." *Jewish Di-al-og* (Passover 1973), pp. 46–47. A brief appraisal of Richler's novels.
Burgess, Anthony. Review of *Cocksure. Life* (15 March 1968), p. 8.
Cameron, Donald. "Mordecai Richler: The Reticent Moralist." *Conversations with Canadian Novelists II.* Toronto: Macmillan, 1973, pp. 114–27. An interview dealing mainly with the later novels.
Cloutier, Pierre. "Mordecai Richler's Exiles: *A Choice of Enemies.*" *Journal of Canadian Fiction* 1 (Spring 1972): 43–49. Examines the political theme of *A Choice of Enemies.*
Cohen, Nathan. "A Conversation with Mordecai Richler." *Tamarack Review,* no. 2 (Winter 1957), pp. 6–23. Interviews Richler before the publication of *A Choice of Enemies.*

————. "Heroes of the Richler View." *Tamarack Review,* no. 6 (Winter 1958), pp. 47–60. Asserts that Richler's insensitivity is reflected in his protagonists.

Cohn-Sfetcu, Ofelia. "Of Self, Temporal Cubism, and Metaphor: Mordecai Richler's *St. Urbain's Horseman.*" *International Fiction Review* 3 (January 1976): 30–34. Examines the temporal element in *St. Urbain's Horseman.*

Cude, Wilfred. "The Golem as Metaphor for Art: The Monster Takes Meaning in *St. Urbain's Horseman.*" *Journal of Canadian Studies* 12 (Spring 1977): 50–69. Considers the symbolic functions of the golem, particularly its artistic and moral significance to Jake Hersh's characterization.

Darling, Michael. "Mordecai Richler: An Annotated Bibliography." *The Annotated Bibliography of Canada's Major Authors.* Edited by R. Lecker and J. David. Downsview, Ontario: ECW Press, 1979. A fairly comprehensive bibliography.

Dooley, D. J. "Mordecai Richler and Duddy Kravitz: A Moral Apprenticeship?" *Moral Vision in the Canadian Novel.* Toronto: Clarke, Irwin, 1979. The central point of dispute of *The Apprenticeship of Duddy Kravitz* concerns Richler's moral attitude to his protagonist.

Edwards, Thomas. Review of *Joshua Then and Now. New York Times Book Review* 85 (22 June 1980): 11, 24–25.

Ferns, John. "Sympathy and Judgement in Mordecai Richler's *The Apprenticeship of Duddy Kravitz.*" *Journal of Canadian Fiction* 3 (Winter 1974): 77–82. Readers' response to Duddy Kravitz oscillates between the sympathetic and the judicial.

Fiedler, Leslie. "Some Notes on the Jewish Novel in English." *Running Man* 1 (July–August 1968): 18–21. Considers Richler's achievement in relation to other Jewish novelists.

Fulford, Robert. Introduction to *The Great Comic Book Heroes and Other Essays by Mordecai Richler.* Toronto: McClelland and Stewart, 1978, pp. 7–10.

Gibson, Graeme. "Mordecai Richler." *Eleven Canadian Novelists.* Toronto: Anansi, 1973, pp. 265–99. An interview which deals with Richler's works, particularly the early novels.

Goodman, Walter. Interview with Mordecai Richler. *New York Times Book Review* 85 (22 June 1980): 11, 22–24.

Greenstein, Michael. "The Apprenticeship of Noah Adler." *Canadian Literature,* no. 78 (Autumn 1978), pp. 43–51. Observes Noah Adler's growth toward affirmation in *Son of a Smaller Hero.*

Kattan, Naim. "Mordecai Richler: Craftsman or Artist." *Canadian Literature,* no. 21 (Summer 1964), pp. 46–51. Offers a brief evaluation of Richler's novels.

Lenoski, Daniel. "In Vindication of Duddy Kravitz." *Études Canadiennes/*

Canadian Studies, 6 (1979). Takes a sympathetic approach to the protagonist.

McSweeney, Kerry. "Revaluing Mordecai Richler." *Studies in Canadian Literature* 4 (Summer 1979): 120–31. Examines Richler's constructive concerns as a satirist and moralist which are undermined by a "deconstructive" negating vision.

Metcalf, John. "Black Humour: An Interview with Mordecai Richler." *Journal of Canadian Fiction* 3 (Winter 1974): 73–76. Discusses the later novels.

Mitcham, Allison. "The Isolation of Protesting Individuals Who Belong to Minority Groups." *Wascana Review* 7 (1972): 43–50. Compares Richler's and Yves Theriault's study of the isolation of minority characters.

Myers, David. "Mordecai Richler as Satirist." *A Review of International English Literature* 4 (January 1973): 47–61. Examines the commingling of satire and pathos in Richler's novels.

Nadel, Ira. "The Absent Prophet in Canadian Jewish Fiction." *English Quarterly* 5 (Spring 1972): 83–92. Includes a brief consideration of Joey as an absent prophet in *St. Urbain's Horseman.*

New, William. "The Apprentice of Discovery." *Canadian Literature,* no. 29 (Summer 1966), pp. 18–33. Includes a critical assessment of *The Apprenticeship of Duddy Kravitz.*

Ower, John. "Sociology, Psychology, and Satire in *The Apprenticeship of Duddy Kravitz.*" *Modern Fiction Studies* 22 (Autumn 1976): 413–28. Examines Duddy Kravitz's character in relation to the Montreal environment and in Freudian terms, while noting Richler's ambivalent attitude toward him.

Pollock, Zailig. "The Trial of Jake Hersh." *Journal of Canadian Fiction,* no. 22 (1978), pp. 93–106. Views the trial at the Old Bailey in *St. Urbain's Horseman* as a metaphor for Jake Hersh's growing self-awareness and confidence.

Ramraj, Victor. "Diminishing Satire: A Study of V. S. Naipaul and Mordecai Richler." *Awakened Conscience: Studies in Commonwealth Literature.* Edited by C. D. Narasimhaiah. New Delhi: Sterling, 1978, pp. 261–74. Includes a study of Richler's satiric tone.

Reid, Verna. "From Anne of G. G. to Jacob Two-Two: A Response to Canadian Children's Fiction." *English Quarterly* 9 (Winter 1976): 11–23. Includes some observations on *Jacob Two-Two Meets The Hooded Fang.*

Ross, Malcolm. Introduction to *The Incomparable Atuk.* Toronto: McClelland and Stewart, 1971, pp. vi–xi.

Sale, Roger. *On Not Being Good Enough.* New York: Oxford University Press, 1979. Has a brief review article on *St. Urbain's Horseman;* sees Richler's narrator as a raconteur.

Sarkar, Eileen. "The Uncertain Countries of Jacques Ferron and Mordecai

Richler." *Canadian Fiction Magazine*, no. 13 (1974), pp. 98–107. Compares Richler's and Jacques Ferron's study of the survival of minority groups in Quebec.

Scott, Peter Dale. "A Choice of Certainties." *Tamarack Review*, no. 8 (1958), pp. 73–82. Shows Richler's development as an artist in *A Choice of Enemies*.

Sheps, David, ed. *Mordecai Richler*. Toronto: Ryerson-McGraw-Hill, 1971. A useful collection of articles on Richler's writings. The editor's introduction provides a thematic survey of Richler's novels up to *Cocksure*.

————. "Waiting for Joey: The Theme of the Vicarious in *St. Urbain's Horseman*." *Journal of Canadian Fiction* 3 (Winter 1974): 83–92. Offers a detailed thematic and structural study of *St. Urbain's Horseman*.

Stovel, Bruce. Introduction to *A Choice of Enemies*. Toronto: McClelland and Stewart, 1977.

Tallman, Warren. "Wolf in the Snow: Part Two." *Canadian Literature*, no. 6 (Autumn 1960), pp. 41–48. Includes an assessment of *The Apprenticeship of Duddy Kravitz*.

————. "Need for Laughter." *Canadian Literature*, no. 56 (Spring 1973), pp. 71–83. Shows how Richler's comic vision orchestrates theme, tone, and structure in *St. Urbain's Horseman*.

Warentin, Germaine. "Cocksure: An Abandoned Introduction." *Journal of Canadian Fiction*, no. 15 (1975), pp. 81–86. Sees *Cocksure* as a moral satire, not just as entertainment or gratuitous black humor.

Woodcock, George. Introduction to *Son of a Smaller Hero*. Toronto: McClelland and Stewart, 1966, pp. vii–xii.

————. *Mordecai Richler*. Toronto: McClelland and Stewart, 1970. A very useful monograph on Richler's writings up to *The Street*.

————. "The Wheel of Fire." *Tamarack Review*, no. 58 (1971), pp. 65–72. A review article on *St. Urbain's Horseman;* Richler synthesizes satire and realism.

Index